FAN
PHENOMENA

DOCTOR
WHO

EDITED BY
PAUL BOOTH

Credits

First Published in the UK in 2013 by Intellect Books,
The Mill, Parnall Road, Fishponds, Bristol, BS16 3JG, UK

First Published in the USA in 2013 by Intellect Books,
The University of Chicago Press, 1427 E. 60th Street,
Chicago, IL 60637, USA

Editor: Paul Booth

Series Editor and Art Direction: Gabriel Solomons

Copy Editor: Emma Rhys

Inside cover images taken at The Doctor Who Experience,
Cardiff Bay © 2012 Visit Wales

A Catalogue record for this book is available from
the British Library

Fan Phenomena Series
ISSN: 2051-4468
eISSN: 2051-4476

Fan Phenomena: Doctor Who
ISBN: 978-1-78320-020-7
ePUB ISBN: 978-1-78320-104-4
ePDF ISBN: 978-1-78320-103-7

Printed and bound by
Bell & Bain Limited, Glasgow

intellect

Contents

Acknowledgements

This book is dedicated to my father, Colin Booth, and my uncle, Gary Booth, who introduced me to *Doctor Who* before I can remember, and whose support I will never forget.

Paul Booth, Editor

Foreword: The Eleven Fandoms?
By Matt Hills

→ **In this 50th anniversary year, it is easy to see *Doctor Who*'s history as split up across eleven different Doctors, each celebrated in a calendar month of 2013 – January through to November – and each promoted via silhouetted designs. But might it also be possible to think about different fandoms that have unfolded across the show's run?**

The first fandom would have involved all those earthly children who greeted the show with wonder and awe in the early Sixties, getting caught up in Dalekmania. This wasn't fandom in the sense of an organized community, but was fandom nonetheless in terms of love for the programme.

And the second fandom? This took loyalty; this meant sticking with the show after changes in production team and after the replacement of every single lead actor, even William Hartnell in the title role. For a programme made up as it went along, *Who* made what Mark Bould calls its ad hoc existence look uncannily like a story arc, eventually revealing that the Doctor's people were out there in the universe, either meddling in planetary affairs or back home on Gallifrey. The second fandom was therefore rewarded with a story arc *avant la lettre*, as an ephemeral, rolling TV drama started to accumulate its own narrative universe.

The third fandom was more closely linked to the establishment of societies; it was all about joining the right club and seeking out like-minded folk. Fandom was beginning to become a socially organized affair, 'official' and recognized by the *Doctor Who* production office – something that would accelerate with the era of fourth fandom. This, though, also introduced highly visible national differences: fourth fandom could watch Tom Baker episodes pretty much on a loop – what Miles Booy calls a chronic hysteresis of seasons – if it was in America. Back in the United Kingdom, fourth fandom started to circulate bootleg recordings, and the moment was prepared for …

The fifth fandom was technologically enhanced: consumer VCR tech meant that now, for the first time, this era of fandom could rewatch and re-view *Doctor Who* as many times as it liked. And along with this technological change, a cultural and industrial change was also on the way: *Doctor Who* was on the verge of becoming cult rather than mainstream television. The sixth fandom, embracing this development, understood *Doctor Who* alongside a range of other telefantasy programmes, with fans catered for by a colourful array of magazines and specialist shops. *Doctor Who*, as James Chapman notes, was drifting away from widespread cultural recognition. Not a decline, as such, but a major contextual change.

The seventh fandom is actually covered by Craig Owen Jones in this volume: it was a fandom of non-TV *Doctor Who*; all those New Adventures and Big Finish audios. 'Hiatus' or 'interregnum' fandom meant becoming a fan of a defunct television series and a legacy brand. The seventh fandom was unlike all others. Not just post-zeitgeist, but post-canon, and *Doctor Who* was whatever fans wanted to nostalgically recreate or progressively reimagine. It was the world of 'trad' and 'rad', new battle lines in skirmishes fought over the worlds of *Doctor Who* beyond television.

All of which gave rise to the eighth fandom: what Alan McKee explores as a hybrid of consumer and producer, fan and professional. By now, fans who had perhaps been children of Dalekmania were cultural producers in positions of power and authority. Post-TV adventures and experiments could be dragged back into 'official' (not just 'licensed')

The Eleven Fandoms?
Matt Hills

media production. For the eighth fandom, *Doctor Who* was a TV programme again – for one night in 1996, but then on a more sustained basis after 2005.

The ninth fandom has been studied by this volume's editor: it is 'digital fandom', a new universe of forums, blogs and wikis. News breaks faster than ever before, and rumours whirl and eddy in the time winds. Episodes are rated, ranked and reviewed mere moments after transmission, as digital fandom represents itself to itself, in real time.

The tenth fandom might be online, but it's still predominantly a material fandom: a fandom of bodies and desires, as Rebecca Williams describes. The tenth fandom writes accomplished fanfic and essays with titles like 'David Tennant's bum' (2012), by Laura Mead, and enjoys scandalizing earlier fan incarnations. The tenth fandom has learnt the rules of being a fanboy and fangirl through other fan cultures and communities, and has brought those rules of engagement into playful, 'shipping activities.

And the eleventh fandom? The book you're reading now is a part of that. Because the eleventh fandom is yet another hybrid; a mix of scholarship and fan attachment, a sense of scholar-fan or aca-fan identity where studying *Doctor Who* means drawing on a passion for The Show, and where fan commentary and (professional) academic commentary start to intermingle and engage in dialogue. In the eleventh fandom, Tat Wood, Paul Magrs and Jonathan Bignell contribute chapters to the same 2007 volume, *Time and Relative Dissertations in Space*; and Paul Cornell, Matt Hills, Kate Orman, Lance Parkin and John Tulloch all write for the same 2009 MIT Press essay collection, *Third Person*. In the eleventh fandom, *Doctor Who* is an object of fascination and theorization all at the same time.

But perhaps there are more than eleven *Doctor Who* fandoms; this sketch is far from exhaustive. And though many of us might have moved with the times, we probably still have a fandom that feels most like *ours*. What is sure, however – and it's the point I really wanted to make via this conceit – is that in terms of fan phenomena, *Doctor Who* is vital, multiple, and open to renewal and rejuvenation at every turn. The twelfth and thirteenth fandoms (whatever they will look like) won't be the end. Here's to all those future fandoms yet to come … ●

GO FURTHER

Books

Love and Monsters: The Doctor Who *Experience, 1979 to the Present*
Miles Booy
(London and New York: I.B. Tauris, 2012)

The Official Doctor Who *Fan Club Volume 1 The Jon Pertwee Years*
Keith Miller
(Raleigh, NC: Lulu Publishing, 2012)

Digital Fandom: New Media Studies
Paul Booth
(New York: Peter Lang, 2010)

Third Person: Authoring and Exploring Vast Narratives
Pat Harrigan and Noah Wardrip-Fruin (eds)
(Cambridge, MA: MIT Press, 2009)

Time and Relative Dissertations in Space: Critical Perspectives on Doctor Who
David Butler (ed)
(Manchester and New York: Manchester University Press, 2007)

Inside the TARDIS: The Worlds of Doctor Who
James Chapman
(London and New York: I.B. Tauris, 2006)

Extracts/Essays/Articles

'David Tennant's bum'
Laura Mead
In Deborah Stanish and L. M. Myles (eds). *Chicks Unravel Time* (Des Moines: Mad Norwegian Press, 2012), pp. 135–44.

'*Doctor Who*: Adaptations and flows'
Mark Bould
In J. P. Telotte and Gerald Duchovny (eds). *Science Fiction Film, Television and Adaptation* (New York and London: Routledge, 2012), pp. 143–63.

'Desiring the Doctor: Identity, gender and genre in online fandom'
Rebecca Williams
In Tobias Hochscherf and James Leggott (eds). *British Science Fiction Film and Television: Critical Essays* (Jefferson, NC: McFarland, 2011), pp. 167–77.

'The child as addressee, viewer and consumer in mid-1960s *Doctor Who*'
Jonathan Bignell
In David Butler (ed). *Time and Relative Dissertations in Space: Critical Perspectives on*

The Eleven Fandoms?
Matt Hills

Doctor Who (Manchester: Manchester University Press, 2007), pp. 43–55.

'How to tell the difference between production and consumption: A case study in *Doctor Who* fandom'
Alan McKee
In Sara Gwenllian-Jones and Roberta E. Pearson (eds). *Cult Television* (Minneapolis: University of Minnesota Press, 2004), pp. 167–86.

Film/Television

Doctor Who [Classic series], Sydney Newman and Verity Lambert, creators (London, UK: BBC, 1963); [New series], Russell T. Davies, creator (Cardiff, UK: BBC, 2005)

~~~~~~

SOMETHING'S INTERFERING WITH TIME, MR. SCARMAN AND TIME IS MY BUSINESS.

~~~~~~

THE 4TH DOCTOR
PYRAMIDS OF MARS

Introduction
Paul Booth

→ I don't know precisely when I became a fan of *Doctor Who* (Newman, BBC, 1963-1989; Segal, BBC/Fox, 1996; Davies, BBC, 2005–present). In fact, I can't really remember a time when I wasn't a *Doctor Who* fan (Figure 1). I grew up near Chicago in the 1980s, when *Doctor Who* was shown on public television on Sunday nights. Those mid-1980s WTTW repeats of the Jon Pertwee, Tom Baker and Peter Davison years helped usher me through childhood, and the Colin Baker and Sylvester McCoy episodes followed me into my teens. I was glued to the set in 1996 for *Doctor Who: The Movie* (Sax). And when I sat down to watch 'Rose' (Boak, Series 1, Episode 1) in 2005, I was instantly transported back to that time in my life when the world was full of wonder and monsters lurked in the shadows.

Fig. 1: The Author (in box) and his father construct the best Halloween costume ever in 1990. (©Gary Booth).

This is a book about the hundreds of thousands of fans that have had similar experiences. And it's a book *for* those fans too. It's a book about the multiple ways that *Doctor Who* fandom is expressed, and about the diverse group of people that call themselves fans. It's a book about what it means to be a fan, and a book about the important lessons fandom can teach. It's a book about the multitudes of fandoms, fan works and fan discussion that *Doctor Who* has generated. Most importantly, it's a book about emotion: the emotional attachment people can feel for a TV show, for the people on that show, and for fellow fans that follow that show.

Indeed, of all fandoms, none are as varied, long-lived and multifaceted as is *Doctor Who* fandom, and both sections of this book are intended to cover a range of topics by asking the questions 'who are *Doctor Who* fans?' and 'what do *Doctor Who* fans do?'. The thirteen chapters in this book explore these questions, with each author offering his/her own interpretation of *Doctor Who* fandom. At the same time, the authors in this book are fans as well, and they all draw on their own rich, fannish experiences.

The first section of the book, 'Who Are *Doctor Who* Fans?', starts off with Ivan Phillips's chapter about nostalgia for the future in the life of a *Doctor Who* fan. He discusses the way the series has, from the start, tapped into the richly nostalgic ideals of family television. Following this, Richard Wallace uncovers the relationship between the production of *Doctor Who* and its fans through his analysis of fan reconstructions of missing episodes. Craig Owen Jones next writes about how fandom survived and thrived in the hiatus years of the 1990s, and then Dylan Morris discusses how New *Who* has helped shape a burgeoning young American nerd culture. Teresa Forde follows this with her discussion of media saturation and the *Doctor Who* Experience in Cardiff, and then I conclude the section by examining fans' first times of viewing *Doctor Who*.

The second half of this book asks 'What Do *Doctor Who* Fans Do?' Leslie McMurtry, Katharina Freund and Brigid Cherry each explore, in their own chapters, how female fans have embraced *Doctor Who* through fanzines, fan vidding and feminine handicrafting, respectively. Denise Vultee explores the lingual background of *Doctor Who* fans through her in-depth look at fans' reconstructions of the Gallifreyan language. Following this, Karen Hellekson uses a reading of the Big Finish *Doctor Who* Unbound series to talk about the way fans can build alternate histories through *Doctor Who*. Finally, both

Introduction
Paul Booth

Jeremy Sarachan and Nistasha Perez discuss the influence of the Internet on fans, and how fans are using social media to both articulate their own fandom, and to create new crossover texts with other cult shows.

Doctor Who fandom is not new; and, indeed, for half a century, *Doctor Who* has given rise to hundreds of thousands of fans. But, of course, *Doctor Who* didn't start out with an enormous fan base: when it premiered on 23 November 1963 it was popular but didn't immediately generate the type of fan reactions we see so clearly today with its New *Who* incarnation. But like its main character, who can regenerate his body and change his appearance, the show developed and changed throughout the years to keep current with contemporary sensibilities (and as Matt Hills shows in his foreword to the book, fandom itself can regenerate as well ...).

As the show aged, so too did its viewers. A strong base of British *Doctor Who* fans developed in the early 1970s, and the introduction of the show to America in the late 1970s and early 1980s brought in a strong American fan audience. And although the critical and mass popularity of the show waned in the 1980s, fan interest only increased. The show went off the air in 1989, but fandom remained with the show throughout the 1990s and 2000s. Through ancillary products, like the Virgin novels (and later the BBC books), the comics and the Big Finish audio plays, *Doctor Who* retained many of its fans and remained in the public consciousness. The television movie in 1996, although failing to secure the television series for which it had been designed, introduced fans to the Eighth Doctor. *Doctor Who* fans even helped enact the rebirth of the series in 2005, as some of the main producers, actors and writers of New *Who* were fans of the Classic series.

A show as long-lived as *Doctor Who* necessarily has to go through changes during its run, and *Doctor Who* has rarely remained static. For the purposes of this book, however, we'll be using consistent terminology to identify the different incarnations of the show. We'll refer to the original *Doctor Who* series (Newman, BBC, 1963–89) as the Classic series and use New *Who* to talk about the New series (Davies, BBC, 2005–present). When a chapter in this book refers to the individual 25- or 45-minute episodes of *Doctor Who* (both Classic and New), we'll use the word 'episode', and in the case of the Classic series, each episode will be considered part of a *story*. Following the nomenclature of the BBC we break Classic *Who* into Seasons (1–26), and New *Who* into Series (1–7, at time of writing).

I've tried to include perspectives of many different types of fans and fan work in this book. But fandom, like the Time Vortex, is infinite. If you're reading through this and you have a different perspective, drop me a line and let me know about it. There's always room for more in this fandom; after all, as Lynne M. Thomas, one of the editors of the 2010 *Chicks Dig Time Lords*, suggests, *Doctor Who* fandom is bigger on the inside ... ●

~~~~~~~~~~

GO FURTHER

Books

Love and Monsters: The Doctor Who *Experience, 1979 to the Present*
Miles Booy
(London and New York: I.B. Tauris, 2012)

TARDISbound: Navigating the Universes of Doctor Who
Piers Britton
(London and New York: I.B. Tauris, 2011)

Triumph of a Time Lord: Regenerating Doctor Who *in the Twenty-first Century*
Matt Hills
(London and New York: I.B. Tauris, 2010)

Chicks Dig Time Lords
Lynne M. Thomas and Tara O'Shea (eds)
(Des Moines: Mad Norwegian Press, 2010)

Running through Corridors
Robert Shearman and Toby Hadoke
(Des Moines: Mad Norwegian Press, 2010)

About Time 1–6
Tat Wood and/or Lawrence Miles
(Des Moines: Mad Norwegian Press, 2004–10)

Tardis Eruditorum
Philip Sandifer
(Amazon.com: CreateSpace Independent Publishing Platform, 2011–)

Science Fiction Audiences
John Tulloch and Henry Jenkins
(London: Routledge, 1995)

Doctor Who: *The Unfolding Text*
John Tulloch and Manual Alvarado
(New York: St Martin's Press, 1984)

Introduction
Paul Booth

Film/Television

Doctor Who [Classic series], Sydney Newman and Verity Lambert, creators (London, UK: BBC, 1963); [New series], Russell T. Davies, creator (London, UK: BBC, 2005)

'Rose', Keith Boak, dir. *Doctor Who* [New series] (Cardiff, UK: BBC, 2005)
Doctor Who: The Movie, Geoffrey Sax, dir. *Doctor Who* [Classic series] (Hollywood, CA: Fox and London, UK: BBC, 1996)

Part 1
Who Are
Doctor Who Fans?

Frock Coats, Yo-Yos and a Chair with a Panda on It: Nostalgia for the Future in the Life of a *Doctor Who* Fan

Ivan Phillips

→ **THE DOCTOR AND THE PRESIDENT**

When I think about my earliest awareness of *Doctor Who* in the early-to-mid-1970s I think, among other things, of textures, the imagined *feel* of material objects (see Figure 1). I think of velvet, silk, metal, wood, leather, wool, felt, paper.

The velvet of the Third Doctor's smoking jackets and Inverness cloaks; the silk of his ruffled shirts; the yellow paintwork and red leather upholstery of his vintage roadster, Bessie; the endless rainbow wool of the Fourth Doctor's scarf; the felt of his broad-brimmed hat and stiff herringbone tweed of his jacket; the rustling white or brown paper from which he offered his jelly babies (which were sometimes dolly mixture); the wood, or *apparent* wood, of the TARDIS exterior. I also think about hair, curly hair, at first white, then dark brown after the shock of regeneration. My own dad had curly hair, at first dark brown, then fading towards white as he approached the shock of his early death. The dark curls were enough, as a child, to enable me to associate my living dad with my fantasy Doctor. Perhaps they are enough, as a middle-aged man, to enable me to associate my fantasy Doctor with my dead dad. Nostalgia's a strange thing, after all; so intimately connected to the physical world but always occurring at the level of emotion.

Recollections of childhood experience are, inevitably, caught in the filters of adulthood – knowledge added, subtracted, modified, warped – and so, when I think about my earliest awareness of *Doctor Who*, the white and the brown curls of my 'original' Doctors become entangled with prior and subsequent Time Lord hairstyles, from the long silver wig of the First Doctor to the floppy 'not ginger' fringe of the Eleventh. The Second Doctor's Beatle cut is especially interesting from the perspective of this chapter. Iconic of the Sixties, it suggests the complex ways in which memory, myth and design have combined over time in the lives of the show. *Doctor Who*, like sexual intercourse (according to the poet Philip Larkin), 'began in nineteen sixty-three'. It also, strikingly, coincided with another emblematic happening of that decade, the assassination of President John F. Kennedy on the day before its first transmission. Coincidence is, in some ways, the essence of nostalgia and the conjunction of these two happenings has long been written into the lore of *Doctor Who*. Take a random sampling of books about the series and it's a safe bet that most of them will mention events in Dallas, Texas, on 22 November 1963, in their early pages. Peter Haining's Doctor Who: *A Celebration*, a book published to celebrate the 20th anniversary of the programme in 1983, is typical in this respect, beginning with a personal reminiscence that consciously fuses incidents: 'I remember that day and those hours vividly. Like countless millions of others I can recall *precisely* where I was and what I was doing when news of that terrible event hit Britain on the Friday evening.' The original broadcast of *An Unearthly Child* (Hussein, 1963, Season 1, Figure 1.2) and the infamy of Lee Harvey Oswald are strangely, inextricably, linked.

Frock Coats, Yo-Yos and a Chair with a Panda on It: Nostalgia for the Future in the Life of a *Doctor Who* Fan
Ivan Phillips

Fig. 2: It began in a junkyard while history was happening elsewhere... The opening scene of An Unearthly Child, 23 November 1963. (Doctor Who ©BBC).

Close association with the shooting in Dealey Plaza has become part of the mythology of *Doctor Who* and might be seen as fixing it in a distinctly 1960s epoch. Haining, for one, goes on to refer to Beatlemania, the Great Train Robbery and the first woman in space, Valentina Tereshkova. There is more to this, however, than a noting of historical coincidence and proximity to memorable cultural landmarks, a kind of significance by association. The post-war era in which *Doctor Who* was created has become a key aspect of its imaginative texture, a fused element within its narrative DNA and the collective awareness of both its fans and a more general audience. In this connection, it's worth recalling that *Remembrance of the Daleks* (Morgan, 1988, Season 25) took the myth back to its own beginnings for its 25th anniversary. Its setting in London, 1963, in and around Coal Hill School and the junkyard at 76 Totter's Lane where it all began, served as a reminder of the programme's rootedness in a particular and conspicuous period. It also indicated the extent to which both the show and the decade that produced it had moved, by then, into the realms of nostalgia. Perhaps suggestively, the first story to return to a contemporary setting after the initial broadcast of *An Unearthly Child* was William Hartnell's third-to-last adventure, *The War Machines* (Ferguson, 1966, Season 3), which made much of a Swinging London backdrop and the newly completed techno-cultural totem of the Post Office Tower. As *Doctor Who* neared the point at which it would build the possibility of endless renewal into its narrative format through the transformation of one actor into another, it also demonstrated an ability to merge a sense of topical 'nowness' with an anticipation of nostalgic spirit.

Doctor Who has lived long enough, and variously enough, for nostalgia *in* the show to merge with nostalgia *for* the show – never more so, perhaps, than in the years when it was 'off air'. From a fan point of view, this means that the 50th anniversary in 2013 celebrates a phenomenon that enables adults to feel a continuation of childhood obsessions, thrills and reassurances, and children to have an enthusiasm that they feel distinct ownership of but can also share with their parents. In the age of social media, video sharing and massively multiplayer online games, this means that *Doctor Who* is able to tap into an ideal nostalgia for family television at the same time as encapsulating the transmedia tendencies of twenty-first-century storytelling.

Junkyard tales
Let's think about that junkyard for a while, because the aim here is to do more than merely restate the 1960s genesis of *Doctor Who*. This is, after all, a show that has limitless travel in time and space as the starting point of its mythology. Part of its genius, and undoubtedly a crucial factor in its longevity and capacity for regeneration, is its fundamental and profound character of *unsettlement*. In plain terms, *Doctor Who* can never be settled in any specific location or era, not even during the main character's exile to

twentieth-century Earth in the early 1970s. So, the date of 23 November 1963 – or of 6 December 1989 or 26 March 2005 – is as significant or insignificant as the fans choose to make it. It took nearly twenty years for the first episode to be novelized but Terrance Dicks's description of the low-key opening scene is richly suggestive: 'Just an incredible mixture of broken-down objects, old cupboards, bits of furniture, dismantled car engines, chipped marble statues with arms and legs and heads missing.' The shadowy clutter and jumble of cultural fragments picked out by the London Bobby's torch might be seen as symbolic of the phenomenon that it introduced, the next item discovered – 'the familiar shape of a police box' – being just another mundane object that somehow doesn't seem mundane any more.

The junkyard tableau with which *Doctor Who* began its 50-year history seems, in retrospect, like a vivid representation of the series itself. The enigmatic hero and his fantastical ship are first encountered in a setting of muddled relics and discarded remnants, an ultra-futuristic concept hidden in an environment primed with a spirit of elegy and nostalgia. This indicates the distinctly 'intertextual' nature of the show, its inherent tendency from the pilot episode onwards to mingle disparate elements, jostling the space-age with the antique. The First Doctor's Edwardian costume is consistent with this and later incarnations have simply varied the theme, with outfits assembled from an eccentrically shuffled wardrobe of western gentlemen's fashion. Tellingly, the costume often presented as the least popular – the Sixth Doctor's garish, mismatched patchwork – is the one that strays furthest from this practice, although even this retains the essential outline of an Edwardian frock-coat, cravat, waistcoat and spats.

Doctor Who has always been as close to costume drama as it is to science fiction. Where it *has* adhered to the traditions of the latter genre, it has been the traditions as defined by Mary Shelley and H. G. Wells. The Gothic aesthetic of the Philip Hinchcliffe years (1974–77), epitomized by 1976's *The Brain of Morbius* (Barry, Season 13), is *Frankenstein* (Shelley, 1818) channelled via Hammer Horror. More generally, these tales from a time machine have a clear indebtedness to the kind of science fiction embodied in the original novella *The Time Machine* (H. G. Wells, 1895). Significantly, Wells has a cameo role in the oft-derided *Timelash* (Roberts, 1985, Season 22), the events of which story supposedly inspire the young Herbert to write his time-travel yarn in the first place. Mary Shelley has herself become a companion of the Eighth Doctor in several recent Big Finish audio productions.

In the context of fandom, these features of the mythos ensure that its appeal is always based, in part, on a sense of prior acquaintance, an awareness of known or half-remembered components reassembled and reimagined in delightfully skewed and idiosyncratic ways. It's revealing, with this in mind, to consider how the trope of the junkyard – the founding trope of the series – has been revisited at least twice since *An Unearthly Child*. In Steve Parkhouse's 'Junkyard Demon', a two-part Doctor Who *Monthly* comic strip from 1981, the Fourth Doctor encounters interstellar scrap merchants, fittingly

Frock Coats, Yo-Yos and a Chair with a Panda on It: Nostalgia for the Future in the Life of a *Doctor Who* Fan
Ivan Phillips

Fig. 3: 'A thing of shreds and patches...' The Cyberman revives in Doctor Who Monthly's 'The Junkyard Demon' (1981). (©Marvel; Doctor Who ©BBC).

named Flotsam and Jetsam, who are reprogramming inactive Cybermen as domestic servants.

For the readership of the magazine at the time of publication, the thrill of seeing the celebrated metal monsters from the television programme was considerable, especially as they had been absent from the screen for over five years. Within six months they would make their surprise return in *Earthshock* (Grimwade, 1982, Season 19), but – beyond its apparent prescience – the most striking feature of 'Junkyard Demon' is its visual representation of its principal cyber-protagonist (Figure 3). The illustrations, by Mike McMahon and Adolfo Buylla, show a Cyberman that is a curious hybrid of design elements from the early evolution of the species, combining the soft face and flash-lamp head-piece of *The Tenth Planet* (Martinus, 1966, Season 4) and the chest unit and distinctive limb tubing of *The Moonbase* and *The Tomb of the Cybermen* (both Barry, 1967, Season 4 and Season 5, respectively). Reassembled and revived in the dilapidation of an outer-space scrapheap, the Cyberman here seems to embody something of the programme itself. A jerry-rigged version of an amalgamated race, it responds to the nostalgia of the fan community, an increasingly powerful and controversial influence during John Nathan-Turner's period as producer. Authors such as James Chapman, in *Inside the TARDIS* (2006), and Brian J. Robb, in *Timeless Adventures* (2009), have suggested that this 'fandom menace' (often personified in the figure of Ian Levine, Nathan-Turner's 'continuity advisor' from 1979 to 1986) was a major contributing factor in the decline and demise of *Doctor Who* in the 1980s. This isn't the place to reopen the discussion, but it's worth considering that the success of the revived series, albeit in a markedly different production context, has been very much a result of (professional) fans rummaging through the figurative junkyard, much as Levine rummaged through actual skips in the late 1970s to recover discarded episodes of the show.

One acclaimed recent story scripted by a fan, Neil Gaiman's 'The Doctor's Wife' (Clark, 2011, Series 6, Episode 4), returns the series to a junkyard location. The Eleventh Doctor follows a distress call to an isolated asteroid which turns out to be a sentient and parasitic being known as House. House is home to Auntie and Uncle, creatures patched together from the remains of travellers lured to the asteroid, and there's a sense in which the story itself is a kind of patchwork homage to the history of the show. Another inhabitant, Nephew, is an Ood, effectively a displaced strand within the mythical fabric

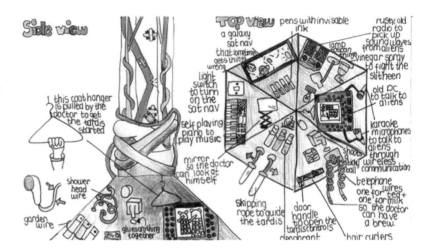

Fig. 4: Susannah Leah's competition-winning design for the junk console featured in 'The Doctor's Wife' (2011). (from the TARDIS Data Core wiki, http://tardis.wikia.com/wiki/File:Susannah_Leah TARDIS_console_design.jpg; Doctor Who ©BBC).

of the New series – especially interesting when it is considered that he was *not* an Ood in Gaiman's original script. The final House-dweller, Idris, is a young woman of Victorian appearance who takes on the matrix or 'soul' of the TARDIS.

House is characterized as an intelligent, malignant rubbish dump, composed from the accumulated, plundered debris of millennia. It can be seen, perhaps, as a perverse and nightmarish metaphor of fandom, including as it does a cupboard full of Time Lord message cubes – the ghostly voices of an extinct race – and a vast TARDIS graveyard. Gaiman's indication during an interview for Doctor Who *Magazine* (*DWM*) that early drafts associated House with the Great Intelligence, from the Troughton era stories *The Abominable Snowmen* (Blake, 1967, Season 5) and *The Web of Fear* (Camfield, 1968, Season 5), tends to reinforce this impression. Interestingly, the Great Intelligence *has* now been reintroduced to the series, initially in the 2012 Christmas Special, 'The Snowmen' (Metzstein, 2012, Series 7, Episode 6), and subsequently in 'The Bells of St John' (McCarthy, 2013, Series 7, Episode 7) and 'The Name of the Doctor' (Metzstein, 2013, Series 7, Episode 13).

At the heart of the episode the Doctor and Idris – a walking, talking, emoting and *dying* embodiment of his 'old girl' – construct a homemade and temporary TARDIS from cannibalized components. The ersatz console was designed as part of a *Blue Peter* (Blair, BBC, 1958–present) competition by a schoolgirl fan, Susannah Leah, working to a brief focused on the use of 'household objects' (Figure 4). That a toy version of Leah's improvised junk console should have been marketed subsequently as one of the popular Character Options range of playsets is a further indication of the rich, complex dialogue between the show, its history and its fans that distinguishes 'The Doctor's Wife'.

Chance encounters
Gaiman's tale exemplifies the steampunk aesthetic that has come to typify *Doctor Who* since Steven Moffat took over from Russell T. Davies as lead writer and executive producer in 2008. Evident in Edward Thomas's 'Heath Robinson' re-design of the TARDIS console for 'The Eleventh Hour' (Smith, 2010, Series 5, Episode 1) – incorporating a typewriter, hot and cold taps, a bakelite telephone, a telegraph and a gyroscope – this is taken to an extreme of absurdity in 'The Lodger' (Morshead, 2010, Series 5, Episode 1), in which the Doctor constructs a scanner from components including a bicycle wheel,

Frock Coats, Yo-Yos and a Chair with a Panda on It: Nostalgia for the Future in the Life of a *Doctor Who* Fan
Ivan Phillips

———

Fig. 5: The homepage of the rather fine 'Chair with a Panda on it' fan blog. (©chairwithapand.wordpress. com).

a lampshade and an umbrella. Relishing the theatrical in-congruity of juxtaposed objects, this recalls the famous line from Lautréamont's *Les Chants de Maldoror* (*The Song of Maldoror*, 1869) in which a young boy is described as being 'as beautiful as the chance encounter of a sewing machine and an umbrella on a dissecting table'. Often used as a shorthand for the spirit of surrealism, the phrase has considerable resonance in the history of *Doctor Who*, notably in relation to moments such as this, from *The Time Meddler* (Camfield, 1965, Season 2):

STEVEN: Look, Doctor, I've seen some spaceships in my time – admittedly, nothing like this, but … Well, what does *this* do?
DOCTOR: That is the dematerializing control and that over yonder is the horizontal hold. Up there is the scanner, those are the doors, that is a chair with a panda on it. Sheer poetry, dear boy! Now, please stop bothering me.

This exchange sparkles with an early and witty celebration of the show's essentially absurdist *mise-en-scène* (Figure 5).

Alongside the panda – delightfully 'random', in the teen-speak of the twenty-first century – is a reference to the television technology of the time, the 'horizontal hold' being one of the manual controls for synchronizing the timebase circuits, usually located at the back of the set. The effect here is to merge the otherworldly technology of the Doctor with the familiar domestic hardware of the viewing audience. The fact that the monitor of the Eleventh Doctor's initial TARDIS console has the look of a 1950s television and is marked as a product of Magpie Electricals is similarly evocative. Magpie Electricals, the Muswell Hill shop at the heart of 'The Idiot's Lantern' (Lyn, 2006, 7), has become a running joke within the series, the brand featuring on such devices as the *Titanic*'s microphone ('The Voyage of the Damned' [Strong, 2008, Series 4, Christmas Episode]), Martha Jones's television ('The Sound of Drums' [Teague, 2008, Series 3, Episode 12]), and River Song's handheld scanner ('Day of the Moon' [Haynes, 2011, Series 6, Episode 2]). The joke has thematic significance, of course, and is embedded within the architecture of Starship UK in 'The Beast Below' (Gunn, 2010, Series 5, Episode 2), a trademark episode in establishing the retrofuturist atmosphere of the Moffat era. The magpie instinct of *Doctor Who*, manifest from the beginning, has now become an explicit recurring motif.

The magic of *Doctor Who* is that its format has always allowed eccentric and extreme fantasy to co-exist with a unique accessibility and imitability of characters, costumes, props and monsters. Children can make a TARDIS out of a cardboard box; they can be a Dalek with an egg whisk, a sink plunger and a grating voice; they can knit a long scarf or wear a bow tie; they can offer jelly babies from a paper bag; develop their skills with a yo-yo. This aspect of the programme's relationship with its fans is captured sharply by

Fig. 6: 'It's smaller on the outside...' A new nostalgia in 'The Snowmen' (2012). (Doctor Who ©BBC).

Paul Magrs in his 2010 novel for teenagers, *The Diary of a* Doctor Who *Addict*, not least in the scene where the young hero, David, realizes that his best friend Robert no longer shares his passion for 'The Show':

He's laughing in the *Doctor Who* exhibition. For a second it seems as shocking as laughing in church. He laughs at a display of model spaceships that have been used over the years. 'You can see what they're made out of,' he says. 'Washing-up liquid bottles. Shampoo bottles. Bits of Airfix plane kits! Sticky-backed plastic!'
I stare at the fake spaceships and think: But we *know* that! That's the point! Someone's spent hours making them out of very ordinary things. That's what I love about them. I love the fact that stuff in space comes from stuff you'd find in your own kitchen at home.

We might recall, at this point, that the Doctor himself made a time flow analogue out of 'very ordinary things' in *The Time Monster* (Bernard, 1972, Season 9), using a cup of tea, a wine bottle, a set of keys and two forks.

Reflecting on such fantastic adaptations of the mundane, it's no coincidence that popular disparagement of the Doctor's greatest enemies, the Daleks, should so often take the form of mocking references to domestic objects and architecture: they are 'dustbins' or 'pepperpots', they (in a now outdated analysis) 'can't even climb stairs'. Such jibes are, of course, part of the story world itself – 'If you're supposed to be the superior race of the universe, why don't you try climbing after us?' taunts the Fourth Doctor in *Destiny of the Daleks* (Grieve, 1979, Season 17) – and they enhance rather than diminish the brilliance of Terry Nation's conception and Raymond Cusick's design.

Intriguingly, the new TARDIS console (Figure 6) revealed in 'The Snowmen' and designed by Michael Pickwoad, shows a movement away from steampunk and towards a more metallic science fiction appearance. This is effectively a shift from one nostalgic register to another, with many fans commenting approvingly on Pickwoad's homage to Peter Brachacki's original console from the Classic series.

Like a police box
Doctor Who encouraged cosplay before cosplay existed, embodying steampunk before the term was coined. It made nostalgia futuristic and a future fit for nostalgia. This is

Frock Coats, Yo-Yos and a Chair with a Panda on It: Nostalgia for the Future in the Life of a *Doctor Who* Fan
Ivan Phillips

reflected in both the titles and the content of Toby Hadoke's successful one-man shows *Moths Ate My* Doctor Who *Scarf* (2006) and *My Stepson Stole My Sonic Screwdriver* (2012), and of Nick Griffiths's memoir *Dalek I Loved You* (2007). There are some parallels here, perhaps, with the more recent Harry Potter phenomenon, another strangely nostalgic mythology generating a similarly obsessive fan community. The extreme commercialization of Rowling's novels following the Warner Brothers film sequence continues to co-exist with a culture of home-whittled wands and home-knitted jumpers. More than any other enduring modern myth, though, *Doctor Who* seems to have contained, in its origins, the elements of a unique narrative and aesthetic that would ensure both a tenaciously loyal primary fan base and the potential for a new one in the twenty-first century. The success of the revived series since 2005 testifies to this, achieving a remarkable balance of classic elements and innovations, honouring deep (and deeply felt) traditions at the same time as embracing the possibilities of contemporary technologies, scenarios, narratives.

Griffiths's remembrance of his own introduction to the programme with Jon Pertwee's arrival in 1970's *Spearhead from Space* (Martinus, Season 7) suggests that this intriguing parent–child fan dynamic is not quite as new as we might think. His elderly father tells him that he was partly drawn to the programme during the Hartnell and Troughton era because the TARDIS reminded him of his own mother, who 'used to make sandwiches for the beat Bobbies (including his stepfather) back in the twenties'. Delivered by Griffiths' father, these would then often be eaten in the seclusion of a local police box.

Spotting this blast from the past in a BBC television series was one enticement for him to watch. Mine was far less nostalgic. I had seen nothing of anything that occurred in *Doctor Who* before. It was all utterly new, a seismic blow to the mind, such a giant leap for my imagination that I was instantly hooked.

In this sense, *Doctor Who* – in 1963, in 1970, in 2013 – does nothing less than tap into a nostalgic ideal of family television itself. It also epitomizes the more general potentials of fiction to reassure, challenge, enrich and transform. As Magrs's David reflects, considering not only his prized collection of Target novelizations but also his other reading:

I do that – I read books and think: that's like him, or that's like her. I'm looking for things I recognise in everything I read. I want to feel at home in these books I pick up. I want them to be more familiar than home and ordinary life. I think that's because I can pick them up and carry them with me. I always have the safe dimension of the book to escape into. Books are bigger on the inside than on the out, just like a police box. ●

~~~~~~~~~~

GO FURTHER

Books

The Doctor's Monsters: Meanings of the Monstrous in Doctor Who
Graham Sleight
(London and New York: I.B. Tauris, 2012)

Love and Monsters: The Doctor Who *Experience, 1979 to the Present*
Miles Booy
(London and New York: I.B. Tauris, 2012)

The Diary of a Doctor Who *Addict*
Paul Magrs
(London: Simon and Schuster, 2010)

Timeless Adventures: How Doctor Who *Conquered TV*
Brian J. Robb
(Harpende: Kamera Books, 2009)

Doctor Who
Jim Leach
(Detroit: Wayne State University Press, 2009)

Dalek I Loved You
Nick Griffiths
(London: Gollancz, 2007)

Time and Relative Dissertations in Space: Critical Perspectives on Doctor Who
David Butler (ed)
(Manchester and New York: Manchester University Press, 2007)

Inside the Tardis: The Worlds of Doctor Who
James Chapman
(London and New York: I.B. Tauris, 2006)

Doctor Who: *A Complete and Utterly Unauthorised Guide*
Mark Campbell
(Harpenden: Pocket Essentials, 2003)

**Frock Coats, Yo-Yos and a Chair with a Panda on It: Nostalgia for
the Future in the Life of a *Doctor Who* Fan**
Ivan Phillips

Fan Cultures
Matt Hills
(London and New York: Routledge, 2002)

Doctor Who: *The Key To Time – A Year-by-Year Record*
Peter Haining
(London: W. H. Allen, 1984)

Doctor Who: *A Celebration – Two Decades Through Time and Space*
Peter Haining
(London: W. H. Allen, 1983)

Doctor Who: *The Unfolding Text*
John Tulloch and Manuel Alvarado
(Basingstoke: Macmillan, 1983)

An Unearthly Child
Terrance Dicks
(London: Target, 1981)

**Online
Websites**

Chair with a Panda on it, chairwithapanda.wordpress.com
Blogtor Who, blogtorwho.blogspot.com

Film/Television

Doctor Who [Classic series], Sydney Newman and Verity Lambert, creators (London, UK:
BBC, 1963); [New series], Russell T. Davies, creator (Cardiff, UK: BBC, 2005)
Blue Peter, John Hunter Blair, creator (London, UK: BBC, 1958)

'The Name of the Doctor', Saul Metzstein, dir. *Doctor Who* [New series] (Cardiff, UK: BBC, 2013)
'The Bells of Saint John', Colm McCarthy, dir. *Doctor Who* [New series] (Cardiff, UK: BBC, 2013)
'The Snowmen', Saul Metzstein, dir. *Doctor Who* [New series] (Cardiff, UK: BBC, 2012)
'The Doctor's Wife', Richard Clark, dir. *Doctor Who* [New series] (Cardiff, UK: BBC, 2011)
'Day of the Moon', Toby Haynes, dir. *Doctor Who* [New series] (Cardiff, UK: BBC, 2011)
'The Lodger', Catherine Morshead, dir. *Doctor Who* [New series] (Cardiff, UK: BBC, 2010)
'The Beast Below', Andrew Gunn, dir. *Doctor Who* [New series] (Cardiff, UK: BBC, 2010)
'The Eleventh Hour', Adam Smith, dir. *Doctor Who* [New series] (Cardiff, UK: BBC, 2010)

'The Voyage of the Damned', James Strong, dir. *Doctor Who* [New series] (Cardiff, UK: BBC, 2008)
'The Sound of Drums', Colin Teague, dir. *Doctor Who* [New series] (Cardiff, UK: BBC, 2008)
'The Idiot's Lantern', Euros Lyn, dir. *Doctor Who* [New series] (Cardiff, UK: BBC, 2006)
Remembrance of the Daleks, Andrew Morgan, dir. *Doctor Who* [Classic series] (London, UK: BBC, 1988)
Timelash, Pennant Roberts, dir. *Doctor Who* [Classic series] (London, UK: BBC, 1985)
Earthshock, Peter Grimwade, dir. *Doctor Who* [Classic series] (London, UK: BBC, 1982)
Destiny of the Daleks, Ken Grieve, dir. *Doctor Who* [Classic series] (London, UK: BBC, 1979)
The Brain of Morbius, Christopher Barry, dir. *Doctor Who* [Classic series] (London, UK: BBC, 1976)
The Time Monster, Paul Bernard, dir. *Doctor Who* [Classic series] (London, UK: BBC, 1972)
Spearhead from Space, Derek Martinus, dir. *Doctor Who* [Classic series] (London, UK: BBC, 1970)
The Web of Fear, Douglas Camfield, dir. *Doctor Who* [Classic series] (London, UK: BBC, 1968)
The Abominable Snowmen, Gerald Blake, dir. *Doctor Who* [Classic series] (London, UK: BBC, 1967)
The Tomb of the Cybermen, Morris Barry, dir. *Doctor Who* [Classic series] (London, UK: BBC, 1967)
The Moonbase, Morris Barry, dir. *Doctor Who* [Classic series] (London, UK: BBC, 1967)
The Tenth Planet, Derek Martinus, dir. *Doctor Who* [Classic series] (London, UK: BBC, 1966)
The War Machines, Michael Ferguson, dir. *Doctor Who* [Classic series] (London, UK: BBC, 1966)
The Time Meddler, Douglas Camfield, dir. *Doctor Who* [Classic series] (London, UK: BBC, 1965)
An Unearthly Child, Warris Hussein, dir. *Doctor Who* [Classic series] (London, UK: BBC, 1963)

Audio

Toby Hadoke, *My Stepson Stole My Sonic Screwdriver* (2012)
Toby Hadoke, *Moths Ate My* Doctor Who *Scarf* (2006)

Other

'Annus Mirabilis'
Philip Larkin
1967

Chapter
02

Joint Ventures and Loose Cannons: Reconstructing *Doctor Who*'s Missing Past

Richard Wallace

→ Towards the end of 1981, Doctor Who *Magazine (DWM)* published a winter special containing a survey of the current state of *Doctor Who* in the BBC's archives. Although some fans were aware that not all of the Doctor's adventures still existed, the article was perhaps the first time that fans were faced with the true extent of the crisis, when BBC archivist Sue Malden listed the 136 episodes of the programme - all from the show's black-and-white era - that were missing or incomplete.

In fact, Malden actually underestimated the problem, as one episode (Episode 1 of the Patrick Troughton adventure *The Invasion* [Camfield, 1968, Season 6]) is incorrectly listed as being held by the BBC. *Doctor Who* fan and historian Richard Molesworth has noted the shock that the publication generated at the time, suggesting that the 1981 winter special 'seemed to be the catalyst that triggered a seismic shift within *Doctor Who* fandom' as fans suddenly 'seemed more focused on the programme's past glories [...] than on the new material being offered up by the BBC'.

For many fans, the missing episodes have become a central part of the show's mythology, and dedicated searches and lucky discoveries have reduced the total number of missing episodes to 106. However, the fascination with *Doctor Who*'s missing past has generated a huge amount of activity beyond the search for these episodes. Most notably in this regard is the continuing fan practice of creating 'reconstructions': video productions which combine a range of audio-visual materials in an attempt to create a version of the missing episodes that can be 'watched'. These reconstructions typify the kinds of fan activity frequently theorized by the academy. In 'The cultural economy of fandom' (1992), John Fiske suggests that most audiences of popular culture 'engage in varying degrees of semiotic productivity', that is, the process of interpreting meaning from a given object. Fans, however, 'often turn this semiotic productivity into some form of textual production that can circulate among - and thus help to define - the fan community'. In most cases this involves '[f]andom [offering] ways of filling cultural lack', producing texts, objects and artefacts as 'a form of cultural labor to fill the gaps left by legitimate culture'. The reconstruction of missing episodes of *Doctor Who* continues such fan behaviour, complicating the relationship - and collapsing the distinction - between official producers and fan creators.

Most frequently taking the form of activities such as writing fanfiction or producing fanvids (see both Leslie McMurtry's and Katharina Freund's chapters in this book), in most cases these endeavours are designed to fill perceived gaps or smooth over narrative inconsistencies, as a way of making sense of a chosen object. Since every existing episode of *Doctor Who* is available on either official BBC VHS or DVD, there is no longer a barrier to audiences who want to gain access to their favourite episodes; a tenth-generation pirate VHS copy of *The Sensorites* (Pinfield & Cox, 1964, Season 1) acquired via fan trading networks is no longer anybody's idea of a Holy Grail, as it might have been in the mid-1980s. Therefore, with every surviving episode readily available to view, interest necessarily turns to those that aren't. Reconstructing missing *Doctor Who* episodes, then, is a particularly literal form of this kind of fan production, given that the endeavour involves plugging 'actual' (rather than perceived) gaps in the programme's archive. In this regard it is not insignificant that the boom in reconstruction production began in the mid- to late 1990s when the show's absence from television screens created a further void to be filled. As *Doctor Who* historian Richard Bignell noted in 1999:

Joint Ventures and Loose Cannons:
Reconstructing *Doctor Who's* Missing Past
Richard Wallace

Fig. 1: Comparing the reconstructions with the real thing: a sequence from The Underwater Menace (1967) as depicted by Joint Venture (left), Loose Cannon (centre) and in a still from the actual episode recovered in 2011 (right). (©Joint Venture; ©Loose Cannon; Doctor Who ©BBC).

with no new televisual material on which to focus, fandom has been presented with a golden opportunity to take a retrospective look at the object of its interest – a chance to look back at what we already have and appreciate it anew, rather than to continually focus on what is immediately ahead.

A wide variety of styles of missing episode reconstructions currently exist (see Figure 1). Most recently, CGI renderings and animations (both unofficial fan versions and officially released BBC versions) have become popular. However, what might best be called the 'typical' version of a *Doctor Who* reconstruction involves matching the soundtrack of the missing episodes with photographic images. As with the reconstructions themselves, the history of how each of these audio-visual components comes to exist is to a great extent dependent on a combination of fan activity, as well as the medium specificity of broadcast television.

The one aspect common to all *Doctor Who* reconstructions is their use of the original soundtracks to the missing episodes, by which I mean a direct recording of all of the sonic aspects of a broadcast, dialogue and all, not just the music. The existence of these soundtracks can be linked to a pre-VHS approach to filling cultural and technological lack. Before the age of home video recorders, television was, perhaps, the ultimate ephemeral cultural object; programmes were broadcast as part of the daily scheduled flow of television, and then were gone. Until the 1960s, many programmes were performed and broadcast live, and even if they were broadcast from a pre-recorded video or film source (as was the case with *Doctor Who*), or tele-recorded upon broadcast, the tapes were frequently reused or destroyed within the space of a couple of years, as Molesworth describes. Regardless of what became of the programmes in the archives, the average television viewer had no way of accessing these recordings even if they did exist, and so ingenuity was required if fans were to be able to re-experience their favourite programmes. For many the solution was to make audio recordings on reel-to-reel (and later cassette) tapes. Seemingly a routine practice for some viewers, a surprisingly large number of *Doctor Who* fans (and fans of other programmes too) recorded episodes in this way. Although many of these tapes were erased, every missing episode of *Doctor Who* survives as an off-air sound recording, and copies of these tapes have been traded amongst fans for decades.

The availability of images from the missing episodes is another product of television's transience. Between 1947 and 1968, a television engineer named John Cura was employed on a freelance basis by BBC production teams, and by individual artists and production staff, to take 'Tele-snaps' of their programmes. These are photographs taken by Cura, using a modified camera, of the images being broadcast live on the screen of his television set. Memos from Cura, held at the BBC's Written Archive Centre (WAC), show that he used the ephemerality of television as part of his sales pitch to the corporation. Of particular note is a 1951 letter to Cecil McGivern, the BBC's Head of Pro-

Fig. 2: A comparison of reconstructions 1: The Change of Identity version of The Savages (1966) (left) includes the complete script, whilst the Loose Cannon version (right) features scrolling descriptive text. (©Change of Identity; ©Loose Cannon; Doctor Who ©BBC).

Fig. 3: A comparison of reconstructions 2: The Joint Venture version of Fury From the Deep (1968) (left) includes static text captions as opposed to Loose Cannon's scrolling text (right). The difference in image quality is noticeable, as is the content of the scene descriptions. (©Joint Venture; ©Loose Cannon; Doctor Who ©BBC).

grammes, which suggests that buying Tele-snaps of BBC productions would provide 'a permanent pictorial record for valuable reference in years to come, of screenings which have a brief life of an hour or so and are then lost for ever unless they have been Tele-filmed'. Cura soon began to sell – and be commissioned to supply – sets of photographs covering whole episodes of individual series. Many production offices, including those for *Doctor Who*, *Z Cars* (Martin and Prior, BBC, 1962–1978) and *Maigret* (Simenon, BBC, 1960–1963) effectively had Cura on a rolling contract to photograph all of their output.

Only a fragment of Cura's work survives, however the WAC does hold Tele-snaps for almost every episode of *Doctor Who* between Episode 1 of *The Gunfighters* (Tucker, 1966, Season 3) and Episode 3 of *The Mind Robber* (Maloney, 1968, Season 6). These were published by *DWM* in a serialized form following their discovery in 1993. However, as Bignell and Lewisohn explain, exhaustive fan activity has continued its attempts to fill the gaps in this visual archive, and in addition to those held by the BBC, a number of other sets of Tele-snaps from otherwise missing episodes (including *Marco Polo* [Hussein, 1964, Season 1] and *The Crusade* [Camfield, 1965, Season 2]) have been unearthed in the private collections of production personnel.

The first instance of a Tele-snap reconstruction is widely accepted to be a version of Episode 2 of *The Power of the Daleks* (Barry, 1966, Season 4) made sometime around 1985 by Richard Landen, one of the fans responsible for the recording of the missing-episode soundtracks in the 1960s and later a writer for *DWM*. However, the production of reconstructions has been most sustained since the mid-1990s, following the publication of the Tele-snaps in *DWM* and advances in desktop computer digital video editing technologies. During the mid-1990s, those individuals involved in producing reconstructions largely arranged themselves into three formal groups: Change of Identity (COI) Joint Venture (JV) and Loose Cannon (LC). Though each group strived for differing levels of fidelity towards the original broadcast, the aim of all three (and those who have followed in their wake) was for fans to be able to experience – in an audio-visual

Joint Ventures and Loose Cannons:
Reconstructing *Doctor Who*'s Missing Past
Richard Wallace

Fig. 4: Two stills from The Wheel in Space (1968) demonstrate the issue of image quality inherent to most reconstructions. The Joint Venture VHS-only version (left) displays severe image degradation, whilst the image quality of Loose Cannon's recent digital version (right) is almost perfect. (©Joint Venture; ©Loose Cannon; Doctor Who ©BBC).

form – those episodes that no longer exist in the BBC's archives.

Each group produced marginally different styles of reconstruction. COI and JV simply combined the Tele-snaps with the audio soundtracks and any surviving clips. However, whereas COI reconstructions included a complete script, exhibited throughout as on-screen captions, JV relied on higher quality Tele-snaps (presented in strict order), and so only used occasional captions to clarify narrative details missing from the soundtrack and images (see Figures 2 and 3). LC is the only one of these three groups still producing reconstructions today, and the team's approach, which utilizes a wide range of existing photographs and footage, augmented with homemade computer animation, suitable extracts from other surviving episodes, newly shot footage and composite photographs, differs substantially from both JV and COI.

Inevitably, such undertakings have held an uneasy relationship with the BBC when it comes to copyright. This has overshadowed all versions of the reconstructions and it is a relationship that has not remained constant. Both the soundtracks and the Tele-snaps are the copyright of the BBC. This was well known by the makers of the reconstructions and so these productions have never been sold or exploited for profit. As the following disclaimer from the LC website highlights, the reconstructions are not intended as alternatives to official BBC products: '*Doctor Who* is the property of The BBC. Nothing on this site intends to infringe upon this copyright. Support The BBC Releases.' Instead, in typical fan-style, the reconstructions have usually been produced in the service of fandom, and distributed via an international group of fan 'dubbers' free of charge, but for the cost of a blank VHS tape and postage. Indeed, it is the use of VHS as a format that ensured the continued success of the project, and it has been frequently suggested by both fans and the reconstructors themselves that the BBC's willing ignorance of the reconstructions has largely been due to their distribution on an analogue format whose image quality would degrade with each successive generation (Figure 4).

The reconstructions were therefore distributed in the same manner that existing episodes had been in the days before the BBC video releases, thus fulfilling a demand which wasn't being met through official channels. This willingness to stay on good terms with the BBC is evidenced by COI and JV's decision to cease producing their reconstructions in the early 2000s, around the time that the BBC began officially releasing the missing episode soundtracks. Concerns that the reconstructions might be competing with official BBC product were made tangible when some of the producers were contacted by Mark Ayres, a former *Doctor Who* composer and the person responsible for overseeing the BBC's range of missing-episode soundtracks, alerting them to BBC concerns about the project.

It is perhaps also significant that this shift in the level of attention aimed at the reconstructions by the BBC coincided with the corporation's own foray into producing officially released reconstructions. Produced by Ralph Montague of the *Doctor Who* Restoration Team (a group of freelance technicians [including Ayres] responsible for digitally re-mastering *Doctor Who* episodes for release on BBC video and DVD since 1997), these official reconstructions generally followed the model established by COI, JV and LC. Indeed, the Restoration Team's website openly acknowledges that for the reconstruction of Episode 4 of *The Tenth Planet* (Martinus, 1966, Season 4) 'it was most helpful to have Rick Brindell's [founder of LC] reconstruction to refer to'. By 2005, the gap between fan-created and officially-released product had narrowed further with the release of a DVD box-set entitled *The Beginning*, which contained a half-hour reconstruction of the serial *Marco Polo* as an extra feature. Whereas previous officially-released reconstructions had been produced 'in-house', albeit using fan versions as a guide, the *Marco Polo* reconstruction is significant for being made by Derek Handley, another member of the LC team.

It is also at this point – where the gap between fan and official product had considerably narrowed – that the BBC's desire to hold the fan-made reconstructions at a distance can be seen most clearly. Unlike the notes for *The Tenth Planet*, which openly acknowledge the fan reconstructions, the Restoration Team's production notes for *Marco Polo* simply note that 'it was decided to approach Derek Handley (who had already done a complete amateur recon best not discussed here!)'. Clearly, at this point in time, official rhetoric was less willing to make connections between BBC products and fan-produced artefacts, an attitude that in all likelihood stemmed from the fact that the release of a series of official reconstructions was then a distinct possibility.

This ambivalent relationship between the BBC and the reconstructors had a long-standing history. For example, the reason why the JV reconstructions had higher quality versions of the Tele-snaps than COI was because the editor of *DWM* had seen the group's former work, liked it, and had given the producers direct access to the images, as revealed by members of the various reconstruction teams in a discussion thread on the 'Planet Kembel' Internet forum. The JV team took copies, digitally enhanced them, and then returned cleaned-up versions to the magazine, something Robert Franks, one of the JV team, suggests was 'a mutually beneficial arrangement as [*DWM*] no longer had to clean up [...] the Tele-snaps [...] to hide all the glue stains'. This did, however, mean that out of professional courtesy, JV could not distribute their reconstructions until after the photographs had been officially published by the magazine. The fan producers have, therefore, had a far more complicated relationship with 'official' representatives of the programme than might be superficially apparent, given that they were responsible for the good condition of the final version of many of the photographs published by the officially licensed and sanctioned *DWM*.

This collapsing of distinction between fan and official producer and fan and official product makes it difficult to identify the point at which one becomes the other, and has the result of legitimating such fan activities. The point at which Handley moved from

Joint Ventures and Loose Cannons:
Reconstructing *Doctor Who's* Missing Past
Richard Wallace

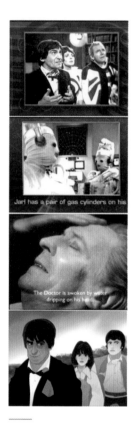

LC producer to BBC producer seems obvious enough, however, that the *Marco Polo* reconstruction remains his only 'official' work for the DVD range suggests that his 'officialization' was temporary. However, the fact that the fan reconstructions were used as the blueprint for the earlier official BBC releases of *The Tenth Planet, The Ice Warriors* (Martinus, 1967, Season 5) and a Tele-snap version of *The Power of the Daleks* released as a multimedia CD, also complicates matters given that the producers involved in those releases may well have been part of the fan communities trading the reconstructions in the first place.

This cross-pollination of fan and official talent is not an uncommon one, and is certainly in line with current trends in the post-2005 television version of *Doctor Who*, where many of the writers, producers and performers were fans of the show during the 1970s and 1980s, became fan producers of one sort or another during the 1980s and 1990s, and have now become part of the official process of *Doctor Who* production. One example of such a trend is Nick Briggs, who played the Doctor in a series of fan-produced and traded audios in the late 1980s and early 1990s, but who is now best known as the voice of the Daleks in post-2005 *Doctor Who*.

More recently, the trend in official and unofficial circles has once again been to relax the strictures on the reconstructions (Figure 5). All of the missing soundtracks have now been officially released by the BBC and the majority of the existing Tele-snaps are also available free-of-charge via the official *Doctor Who* website. The 2006 DVD release of *The Invasion*, which included animated versions of the serial's two remaining missing episodes is generally considered to have 'raised the bar' as far as representations of the missing episodes is concerned, and it seems that BBC-created reconstructions are no longer being actively pursued. To some extent this has been officially acknowledged with the release of another animation – this time to complete the William Hartnell story *The Reign of Terror* (Hirsch & Gorrie, 1964, Season 1) – and the announcement of three further animations to come: *The Tenth Planet, The Ice Warriors*, and *The Moonbase* (Barry, 1967, Season 4). It was also reveals that a reconstruction of the 1965 serial *Galaxy 4* (Martinus & Pinfield, 1965, Season 3) was produced, dropped from the release of *The Time Meddler* (Camfield, 1965, Season 2) at short notice, though this has since been included alongside the newly discovered Episode 3 on the Special Edition DVD of *The Aztecs* (Crockett, 1964, Season 1). Since the BBC's decision to stop producing reconstructions, the latest LC productions (which also include large quantities of CGI) are now being distributed via YouTube as well as on VHS, breaking LC's analogue-only policy (see Figure 6). However, so far these digital versions have also seemingly been ignored by the BBC, presumably because fan reconstructions are no longer seen as being in competition with official BBC product.

The missing episode reconstructions, therefore, can be seen as a site on which a number of issues central to fan studies converge. As I have suggested, intense fan activity has been required to produce these artefacts, as well as to create and source the

Fig. 5: The evolution of the BBC's officially released reconstructions can be traced from the cut-down version of The Ice Warriors *(1967) (top) with audio description, the full length Loose Cannon-style* The Tenth Planet *(1966) (second top) and* Marco Polo *(1964) (second bottom) reconstructions, through to the current preference for animation, as with 2006's release of* The Invasion *(1968) (bottom). (©Loose Cannon;* Doctor Who *©BBC).*

Fig. 6: Reconstructions
for the digital age: Loose
Cannon's reconstruction of
The Wheel in Space (1968)
includes numerous CGI
sequences (left). At the same
time YouTube has provided
an outlet for fan producers
to approach reconstructions
in numerous interesting
ways, including user
drwhoanimator's popular
animations of episodes such
as The Power of the Daleks
(1966) (right). (©Loose
Cannon; ©drwhoanimator;
Doctor Who ©BBC).

composite materials in the first place. The tension between fan and official products and producers is highlighted by the shifting attitudes that the BBC has displayed towards the creators of the reconstructions, and complicated by the corporation's recruitment of fan-producers in order to produce official products. Regardless of all of these concerns, one thing is certain: as long as there are missing episodes of *Doctor Who*, there will be some fans attempting to find them, and others attempting to reconstruct them from gradually ageing soundtracks and glue-stained Tele-snaps. ●

GO FURTHER

Books

Wiped! Doctor Who's *Missing Episodes*
Richard Molesworth
(Prestatyn: Telos Publishing, 2010)

Extracts/Essays/Articles

'John Cura – Photographer of the lost archive'
Richard Bignell with Mark Lewisohn
In *Nothing At the End of the Lane – The Magazine of* Doctor Who *Research and Restoration* 2 (June 2005), pp. 11–20.

'From the editors'
Bruce Robinson, Robert Franks and Richard Bignell
In *Nothing At the End of the Lane – The Magazine of* Doctor Who *Research and Restoration* 1 (July 1999), pp. 3–4.

'The cultural economy of fandom'
John Fiske
In Lisa A. Lewis (ed). *The Adoring Audience: Fan Culture and Popular Media* (London and New York: Routledge, 1992), pp. 30–49.

Film/Television

Doctor Who [Classic series], Sydney Newman and Verity Lambert, creators (London, UK: BBC, 1963)

Joint Ventures and Loose Cannons:
Reconstructing *Doctor Who*'s Missing Past
Richard Wallace

Z Cars, Troy Kennedy Martin and Allan Prior, creators (London, UK: BBC, 1962)
Maigret, Georges Simenon, creator (London, UK: BBC, 1960)

The Invasion, Douglas Camfield, dir. *Doctor Who* [Classic series] (London, UK: BBC, 1968)
The Mind Robber, David Maloney, dir. *Doctor Who* [Classic series] (London, UK: BBC, 1968)
The Ice Warriors, Derek Martinus, dir. *Doctor Who* [Classic series] (London, UK: BBC, 1967)
The Moonbase, Morris Barry, dir. *Doctor Who* [Classic series] (London, UK: BBC, 1967)
The Power of the Daleks, Christopher Barry, dir. *Doctor Who* [Classic series] (London, UK: BBC, 1966)
The Tenth Planet, Derek Martinus, dir. *Doctor Who* [Classic series] (London, UK: BBC, 1966)
The Gunfighters, Rex Tucker, dir. *Doctor Who* [Classic series] (London, UK: BBC, 1966)
Galaxy 4, Derek Martinus & Mervyn Pinfield, dir. *Doctor Who* [Classic series] (London, UK: BBC, 1965)
The Time Meddler, Douglas Camfield, dir. *Doctor Who* [Classic series] (London, UK: BBC, 1965)
The Crusade, Douglas Camfield, dir. *Doctor Who* [Classic series] (London, UK: BBC, 1965)
The Reign of Terror, Henric Hirsch & John Gorrie, dir. *Doctor Who* [Classic series] (London, UK: BBC, 1964)
The Sensorites, Mervyn Pinfield & Frank Cox, dir. *Doctor Who* [Classic series] (London, UK: BBC, 1964)
The Aztecs, John Crockett, dir. *Doctor Who* [Classic series] (London, UK: BBC, 1964)
Marco Polo, Warris Hussein, dir. *Doctor Who* [Classic series] (London, UK: BBC, 1964)

Online
Extracts/Essays/Articles

'Joint Venture reconstructions??'
Welshcarroll
Planet Kembel – The Ian Levine Doctor Who *discussion forum*. 29 October 2008, http://ianlevine.forumco.com/topic.asp?TOPIC_ID=5089&whichpage=1

'2/E should give the fans what the fans want'
Gallifrey Base. n.d., http://gallifreybase.com/forum/showthread.php?t=11646

'Loose Cannon and other recons thread'
Gallifrey Base. n.d., http://gallifreybase.com/forum/showthread.php?t=5927

Websites

Fan reconstructions of missing Doctor Who stories [Loose Cannon *Doctor Who* reconstructions], http://www.recons.com
The Doctor Who *Restoration Team Website*, http://www.restoration-team.co.uk
The Disused Yeti newsletter, http://archive.whoniversity.co.uk/dy/dy_main.htm

Other

Memo to Cecil McGivern
John Cura, 1 October 1951, BBC Written Archive Centre, Caversham, File: WAC T15/3/1.

Chapter
03

Life in the Hiatus: New *Doctor Who* Fans, 1989–2005

Craig Owen Jones

→ *Doctor Who* failed to survive the 1980s. The final episode of its 26th season was broadcast on 6 December 1989, and while the BBC avoided making explicit pronouncements to the effect that the programme had been cancelled, no further series were commissioned until 2003, and new *Doctor Who* serials did not see the light of day until 2005, with the appearance of Christopher Eccleston's Ninth Doctor.

The period between the series' de facto cancellation in 1989 and its 2005 relaunch has come to be known in fandom circles as 'the wilderness years', or, more simply, as 'the hiatus'. The latter term will be used here, not only for reasons of brevity, but also because it is suggestive of a gap that compromises the completeness of something – a meaning that has a bearing on our understanding of that subset of *Doctor Who* fans who discovered the programme during that period (hereafter referred to as 'hiatus fans'). Their experience was unlike that of any *Doctor Who* fans before them. By the time the programme had established itself as a staple of British television in the mid-1960s, it had built up a small but dedicated following of fans, and as it progressed beyond its status as a semi-educational children's series, its ambience underwent a series of alterations, characterized by what John Tulloch and Henry Jenkins refer to as 'production signatures' – the adoption of new narrative approaches and plotlines, often associated with changes in producer, as Table 1 demonstrates.

Table 1 **A typology of *Doctor Who* 'production signatures'** (source: *Chapman*)

Producer	Period	Type of story
Verity Lambert	1963–65	'Historical'
Innes Lloyd	1966–68	'Monsters'
Barry Letts	1969–74	'Action adventure'
Philip Hinchcliffe	1974–77	'Gothic horror'
Graham Williams	1977–80	'Comedy'
John Nathan-Turner	1980–89	'Hard science fiction'/ self-reflexivity

During the programme's first run, then, viewers bore witness to incremental changes in the tone of the programme, and it follows that the reactions these changes prompted had a bearing on how they constructed their own identities as fans.

Where, however, does this leave 'hiatus fans'? For them, there was no canonized production signature against which to judge their experiences of the programme (beyond, that is, the stereotypical notions of 'cardboard sets' and 'corridor acting' for which the series was famous in British culture throughout the 1970s and 1980s). For British 'hiatus fans' at least, typically born in the early 1980s but coming of age in the 1990s, the familial milieu in which they might have been introduced to the programme – for those without siblings or friends who were already fans, at least – typically did not exist. In its absence, we must look for other ways in which those who became fans during the hiatus arrived at their fan identity. This chapter, then, will analyse this process, examining issues of identity formation as well as the position of 'hiatus fans' of the Eighth Doctor (Paul McGann) in relation to his place in the universe of *Doctor Who*.

Life in the Hiatus: New *Doctor Who* Fans, 1989–2005
Craig Owen Jones

'Hiatus fans': Discovering *Doctor Who*

What follows is a tentative typology of the methods by which 'hiatus fans' may be demonstrated to have formulated their identities as fans of *Doctor Who*. In distinguishing
between these and earlier fans, I draw upon notions of the 'learning pathway' and the
'acquisition pathway', concepts more commonly found in linguistics to illustrate the
ways in which second languages are learned. As articulated by Keith Johnson, the
'learning pathway' denotes the progression in language proficiency from possessing *declarative* knowledge (i.e. knowing about something, such as a language) to possessing
procedural knowledge (i.e. knowing how to do something, such as speaking a language).
Approaches to language learning that adopt the 'acquisition pathway', meanwhile, turn
this process on its head: the learner, who typically finds him or herself immersed in an
environment where the language they wish to learn is being used, begins with procedural knowledge gained through use, which is then broadened to encompass declarative
knowledge – the learner picks up words, phrases and idioms and repeats them verbatim,
and only later begins the process of understanding *why* they function as they do.

This is an appropriate framework to use when discussing how 'hiatus fans' gain their
fan identity because they can be distinguished from older *Doctor Who* fans in precisely
this way. Before the series' cancellation, the route of viewers towards a fan identity when
no previous contacts with *Doctor Who* or science fiction fandom existed was through
what can be defined as an acquisition pathway. Before the 1980s, *Doctor Who* featured
little explicit referencing of its own history: only one multi-Doctor story, *The Three Doctors* (Mayne, 1973, Season 10), had been screened, and apart from the Daleks, the Master,
and the Cybermen, few other enemies of the Doctor appeared in multiple stories. In the
absence of a narrative framework in which to situate the show's stories and understand
the finer points of its mythology, viewers learnt as they watched, acquiring knowledge
of such tropes as regeneration at first-hand (in 1966, 1969, 1974, 1981, 1984 and 1987,
respectively), and assembling a backstory, composed of (indeed, effectively restricted
to) remembrances of past Doctors and their companions, which later came to be extensively referenced during the 'self-reflexive' era of 1980s *Doctor Who* under producer
John Nathan-Turner.

This invites comparisons with the acquisition pathway of language learning. Until
the 1970s, an era when home recording was a hobby for the rich and before videos of
old serials were commercially available, those wishing to expand their knowledge of the
Doctor Who universe beyond the confines of live TV transmissions of episodes had recourse to published books about the phenomenon, the pages of Doctor Who *Magazine*
(*DWM*), and little else before entering the world of fandom. Therefore, the episodes
themselves – more specifically, *the episodes that were being screened or repeated at
any given time* – served as the primary carrier of the programme's identity.

A good illustration of the acquisition pathway is the fan response to the 1982 serial

Earthshock (Grimwade, Season 19). During the serial, the Cybermen antagonists view brief clips of several previous incarnations of the Doctor – only the second time that footage of any of the previous actors to play the Doctor had been viewed on-screen subsequent to their tenures in the role. Fan reaction to the sequence, as remembered for a documentary included on the serial's DVD release, was emphatic, and is illustrative of the disadvantages of the acquisition pathway; the relative dearth of readily available information on earlier eras of the programme prior to *Earthshock* is obvious: 'I thought I'd died and gone to heaven'; 'to actually have a chance to sit down and see all these tiny little moments [in the show's history] …'; 'I got a sense of the series' past'. For these fans, well versed in the *Doctor Who* of their era, but not in what preceded it, such moments afforded a way of locating their own viewing experiences within the show's larger existence.

For 'hiatus fans', however, this approach can obtain only in circumscribed ways. For those discovering the programme during the hiatus, becoming a fan required a concerted effort that went far beyond maintaining interest during the 'dead time' between seasons endured by fans of previous eras, for there were no new seasons. Rather, these fans actuated their interest in the show via one or more 'learning pathways', the most important of which are described below. (The following concentrates on British audiences only).

Learning pathway 1: Repeat broadcasts
In 1992, with the programme's 30th anniversary approaching, the BBC began repeating *Doctor Who* serials from across the programme's history, including stories featuring all seven Doctors. These repeats were eventually scrapped in 1994 due to poor viewing figures. A further (curtailed) series of repeats was undertaken in 1999. In addition, some serials were later repeated on satellite television.

Learning pathway 2: The 30th anniversary
Popular interest in *Doctor Who* reached a peak in late 1993, with the arrival of the programme's 30th anniversary. A well-received documentary, *Thirty Years In The TARDIS* (Davies), was aired, and the possibility of filming a new *Doctor Who* story was suggested. Although a 90-minute one-off episode was at first mooted, the programme that was eventually commissioned was *Dimensions In Time* (MacDonald), a 13-minute two-part charity special broadcast as part of the yearly Children In Need appeal in November, featuring all five of the Doctors still alive. The programme was given a great deal of advance publicity – a *Radio Times* cover dedicated to it in the week preceding its broadcast was complemented by a live appearance of the Third Doctor, Jon Pertwee, on a special segment of *Noel's House Party* (Edmonds, BBC, 1991–99) for Children In Need immediately preceding the special's transmission.

As a dramatic presentation, *Dimensions In Time* was poorly conceived, featuring

Life in the Hiatus: New *Doctor Who* Fans, 1989–2005
Craig Owen Jones

a crossover – filmed in 3D – between the universes of the Doctor and the soap opera *Eastenders* (Smith and Holland, BBC, 1985–present). However, to those unacquainted with the nuances of the programme, and in spite of its many shortcomings, the ambience of the special, centred as it was on acknowledging *Doctor Who*'s rich history via the inclusion of a dozen former companions as well as a bevy of monsters and archenemies, served as a tantalizing indication of the storytelling possibilities the programme afforded.

Likewise, the staging of events, conventions and exhibitions in the wake of the anniversary, such as the permanent exhibition of props at Llangollen, Wales (1994–2003), and temporary exhibitions such as that at Needles on the Isle of Wight (1994) ensured the programme remained in the public eye to some extent.

Learning pathway 3: The New Adventures and Missing Adventures novels
In 1989, Virgin Books acquired the Target Books imprint that had been responsible for publishing novelizations of *Doctor Who* serials. Following the programme's cancellation, Virgin began to publish the New Adventures, a continuation of the narrative that had ended with the stories of the Seventh Doctor's final season. Later in the decade, the same press began publication of another range of books, the Missing Adventures, featuring the other Doctors. Both ranges proved successful, and prompted BBC Books to issue their own series of novels in the late 1990s (see below). Further novels and novellas were commissioned in the early 2000s.

Learning pathway 4: The Eighth Doctor
In 1996, *Doctor Who: The Movie* (Sax) was premiered. The brainchild of Philip Segal, a British-born American producer, the telefilm was a co-production of the BBC and the Fox network. As the only canonical screen appearance of the Doctor between 1989 and 2005, the television movie is central to any discussion of 'hiatus fans', and will be considered separately below.

Learning pathway 5: Audio dramas
These included two radio serials featuring Jon Pertwee broadcast in 1993 and 1996 respectively; the issuing of newly-discovered fan-made audio recordings of otherwise lost serials from the 1960s; and, from 1999, a highly successful series of audio dramas commissioned by Big Finish Productions (see Karen Hellekson's chapter in this volume).

Learning pathway 6: Online content
To coincide with the programme's 40th anniversary in 2003, the BBC experimented with the production of animated *Doctor Who* stories. The result was *Scream of the Shalka* (Milam), a serial comprising six fifteen-minute episodes, made available on the BBC website from November 2003, and featuring Richard E. Grant as the Ninth Doctor (but

see below).

By a combination of the above, 'hiatus fans' were able to enter the world of *Doctor Who* fandom. Indeed, in formulating their identity, 'hiatus fans' found themselves attempting to negotiate a complex set of obstacles. Much of *Doctor Who* fandom revolves around notions of ownership of particular incarnations of the Doctor. While most *Doctor Who* fans enjoy watching incarnations of the Doctor from before and after the period in which their own identity as fans of the series was formed (typically in childhood or adolescence), and awareness of other eras in the show's history is commonplace, it is nevertheless true that, for many, identification with 'their' Doctor remains the primary method for understanding the show and its concerns. Implicit in this concept is the notion of a 'generational moment': a window in one's life in which a fondness for *Doctor Who* is acquired; and while this cannot hold true for all fans, valorizing one's 'own' Doctor – the Doctor of one's youth – is clearly a fairly typical route into fandom.

However, for 'hiatus fans' – until 1996, at any rate – there was no such figure. Fans accordingly learnt about *Doctor Who before* performing their identities as fans, in a variety of ways: through 'vicarious nostalgia' actuated by repeats, charity specials, and the collecting of commercially available serials, among other methods; identification with the Seventh Doctor (i.e. the character's most recent incarnation); and new media (novels and audio dramas). Nevertheless, the appearance of the Eighth Doctor in the 1996 television movie presented new possibilities for 'hiatus fans', and it is on the significance of this event that the remainder of this chapter will focus.

'Hiatus fans' and the Eighth Doctor

In its approach to narrative, the 1996 telefilm in which McGann's Eighth Doctor makes his one (and so far only) screen appearance uncomfortably straddles the boundary between the Classic and New series.[1] As befits what was intended as a back door pilot for an American-produced version of the show, the first third of the film is expository in nature, establishing the Doctor's ability to regenerate – Sylvester McCoy enjoys a swansong as the Seventh Doctor, accidentally shot in a gang shootout on the streets of San Francisco – as well as the introduction of the TARDIS.

At that point, however, similarities between the television movie and the BBC series end. Peter Wright has recently written about the film as a product of American cultural imperialism: the 'politically liberal' figure of the Doctor is replaced here by a conservative character whose status as an agency of good is symbolized not by a determination to redefine the social order, but by his regeneration (presented as a resurrection from the dead, and filmed so as to allude to Christ's resurrection), and his personal battle with his evil archenemy, the Master. Indeed, for fans of the show, the film's depiction of the Master (Eric Roberts) is particularly jarring. Reimagined as a Terminator-like, leather-clad macho man, his demeanour is completely at odds with that of the Master as played

Life in the Hiatus: New *Doctor Who* Fans, 1989–2005
Craig Owen Jones

Fig. 1: The Eighth Doctor links
to the past, but looks to the
future, in Doctor Who:
The Movie (1996).
(Doctor Who ©BBC)

by Roger Delgado or Anthony Ainley (or, for that matter, John Simm, whose puckish portrayal is arguably closer to Delgado's). Wright sees this character, who draws one of the Doctor's (male) companions to his side in a conversation notable for its homoerotic overtones, as a 'predatory queer' – a reading that, taken with the hetero-sexualization of the Doctor implied by his unprecedented kissing of Grace, his female companion, serves to reinforce the narrative's emphasis on social conservatism, 'a shadow play of abstract notions rather than the political parable an audience familiar with *Doctor Who* might expect'.

Although it achieved respectable viewing figures of around nine million on its United Kingdom premiere in May 1996, and proved a success in terms of merchandizing, *Doctor Who: The Movie* was seen as a critical failure due to its convoluted plot and its overly lengthy exposition. However, for hiatus fans, for whom this represented the first new addition to the programme's canon, certain aspects of the film were doubtless revelatory, such as its look. As Paul Watts has noted, '[the film's] greatest legacy […] is its aesthetics. *Doctor Who* had never looked as good up to this point.' The film's steampunk-influenced TARDIS interior and high-quality special effects – a far cry from the wobbly sets and often risible model shots of the television programme – belied its reputation for poor production values, inviting comparison, as Wright points out, with genre-leading franchises such as *Star Trek* (Roddenberry, CBS, 1966–69). To an extent this perception would have been informed by the various 'production signatures' borne by the show, as Table 1 suggests, depending on each fan's exposure to previous serials. Whatever the fan's previous experience of *Doctor Who*, however, the sophistication of the film's visuals underlined the Eighth Doctor's status as a contemporary figure, albeit one with inalienable links to a rich past.

An equally important factor was the character of the Eighth Doctor himself (Figure 1). The oblique nature of the role of the Doctor has given the actors chosen to play him extraordinary latitude in interpretation, which has consequences not only in terms of tone, but for the show's very meaning. For example, Peter Davison's intensely humanistic portrayal of the Doctor, no less than Sylvester McCoy's increasingly mercurial demeanour, affected the nature of their relationships with both companions and occasional characters, and invited differing audience responses.

Paul McGann's Eighth Doctor contained elements familiar to fans. His flamboyant Edwardian mode of dress drew comparisons with that of the Third Doctor, played by Jon Pertwee in the early 1970s, while his adroitness at sleight of hand recalled the playfulness of Patrick Troughton's Second Doctor. These and other similar elements designed to evoke the atmosphere of the Classic series, while prominent in the film, nevertheless fail in this regard: '[producer Philip Segal] mistakes presence for resonance, [and erroneously] believes the mere appearance of these […] will, in some ambiguous manner, evoke the sensibility of the original program.' Wright's observation here is correct; one cannot deny that the ham-fisted inclusion of the Daleks in the film's spoken-word intro-duction, bizarrely recast as purveyors of justice, grated with those who were completely conversant with the programme's past.

However, by the same token one might equally suggest that for 'hiatus fans', pres-ence could indeed equate to resonance. Lacking experienced understanding of the universe of *Doctor Who*, the anachronistic appearance (for example) of jelly babies and a sonic screwdriver in the Seventh Doctor's opening scenes, while jarring to other fans (the Seventh Doctor was associated with neither during the TV series), may instead have provided 'hiatus fans' with validation that they were bearing witness to a new instalment in an ongoing narrative. Knowledge of the Fourth Doctor's predilection for jelly babies, and the ubiquity of the sonic screwdriver (before its destruction during a 1982 serial), are among the commonest received notions of the Doctor's persona, and to 'hiatus fans' were therefore arguably more important as markers of the programme's identity than notions of in-universe continuity (at least, until they became more acutely aware of that continuity). It may be suggested that for these fans, the telefilm represented a sort of initiation into the Doctor's world – a world that, with its TARDIS, its beautiful female companion, and an enemy known even to the greenest of initiates, connected the current act of viewing with previous acts of viewing, and in so doing, was itself a way of allowing them to perform their newly-acquired identities as fans.

Given the production's shortcomings, it is unsurprising that it was the amiability of McGann's portrayal that figured highly in sympathetic appraisals. McGann's Doctor was widely admired in fan circles, even as the film itself was lambasted. For our purposes, it is interesting to note that the Eighth Doctor, effectively identified in the New series as a participant in the 'Time War' that occupies such a central role in the *Doctor Who* universe, gained a small but vibrant community of fans in his own right; indeed, the 'Half Human Doctor' messageboard, established in early 2008, features a wide range of fanfiction largely derived from scenarios and story arcs from the Eighth Doctor's novels and audio dramas, and McGann himself regularly makes appearances at *Doctor Who* conventions to appreciative audiences.

Conclusion: 'Hiatus fans' and the Eighth Doctor's canonicity
The disparity between the storytelling agendas of the Classic and New series which the Eighth Doctor exemplifies, the problematic issue of his 'half-human' nature (a revela-tion inconsistent with the character's established backstory), and the brevity of his sole appearance in the telefilm, as well as its failure to produce a new series, do not seem to constitute an insurmountable barrier to acceptance of his canonical status. As Piers Britton has noted, 'the narrative [of *Doctor Who*] has accommodated so many altera-tions in ideology and taste without recourse to such devices as *Star Trek*'s introduction of 'next generation' and 'prequel' series, and without any absolute rupture in consisten-

Life in the Hiatus: New *Doctor Who* Fans, 1989–2005
Craig Owen Jones

Fig. 2: Richard E. Grant played an alternate Ninth Doctor in 'The Scream of the Shalka' (2003). (Doctor Who ©BBC)

cy'. In spite of the fact that McGann's Doctor is on-screen for less than an hour – by far the briefest sojourn of any Doctor – it is the mere fact of that appearance, combined with the way in which his story is intertwined with that of the Seventh Doctor, which bestows canonical status on the character. The point is underlined by the fate of Richard E. Grant's aforementioned 'Shalka Doctor' (2003), who was at one time feted by the BBC as the (canonical) Ninth Doctor (Figure 2); that status was revoked in short order once the new TV series had been commissioned, a decision that is of relevance because it aroused no dissension whatsoever in fan circles. Clearly, the appearance of an actor in live action over-rode considerations of precedence.

However, there is another, unexplored possibility that may have a bearing on the issue: the presence in the audience of 'hiatus fans' – for whom the Eighth Doctor's emergence was immediate, momentous (because the first to be witnessed 'at the time'), and novel – bestowed legitimacy on the character, because they provided that missing element that had hitherto been a staple and obvious component in the programme's demographic: *a new generation of fan*. At least one fan writer, Margaret Brown, has written in similar terms, though with caveats. Noting that although the movie did no more than light 'the fledgling flame of my [fan identity] [...] one movie doesn't make a fanatic', she nevertheless considers herself 'a child of the Eighth Doctor', having been drawn to the telefilm during her adolescence in the mid-1990s. However, for Brown, what marked her experience out from that of older fans was the absence of *Doctor Who* in the cultural discourse of the 1990s as she experienced it, leading her to identify herself as 'part of the lost generation of *Who* fans':

My first doctor was Paul McGann. [...] I can't help feeling that I've missed out on something. I can't have a lunchbox, a thermos, collect stickers or buy a magazine that offers free cut-out masks and drawing competitions. I can't have a Dalek bedspread or Cybermen curtains [...] I could purchase all of these items but it's not the same as being young and drawn in by it all. [...] I can't even buy all the stuff and relive my youth through it, because it wasn't my youth.

Although demonstrating that there is a body of fans who, like Brown, consider the Eighth Doctor to be 'their' Doctor lies outside the scope of the present discussion, the very fact that writers such as Brown can so wistfully describe the inadequacies of their 'generational moment', yet are still able to refer to McGann as 'theirs', is important. Their alacrity in identifying as fans - not merely during, but *of* this difficult period in *Doctor Who*'s history – is a not insignificant factor in the Eighth Doctor's story, and in his continued popularity. ●

Notes
1. A split second 'live' appearance in the 2013 episode 'The Name of the Doctor' (Metzstein, 2013, Series 7, Episode 13) notwithstanding; the Eighth Doctor was played on that occasion by an extra. *Momentary* appearances of the Eighth Doctor, in the form of flashbacks, occur in 'The Next Doctor' (Goddard, 2008, Specials, Episode 1) and 'The Eleventh Hour' (Smith, 2010, Series 5, Episode 1).

~~~~~~~~~~~~~

GO FURTHER

Books

TARDISbound: Navigating the Universes of Doctor Who
Piers Britton
(London and New York: I.B. Tauris, 2011)

Inside The TARDIS: The Worlds of Doctor Who
James Chapman
(London and New York: I.B. Tauris, 2006)

An Introduction to Foreign Language Learning and Teaching
Keith Johnson
(Harlow: Pearson, 2001)

Science Fiction Audiences: Watching Doctor Who *and* Star Trek
John Tulloch and Henry Jenkins
(London and New York: Routledge, 1995)

Extracts/Essays/Articles

Untitled article on *Doctor Who: The Movie*
Paul Watts
Panic Moon 7 (January 2012), n.p.

'Expatriate! Expatriate! *Doctor Who: The Movie* and commercial negotiation of a multiple text'
Peter Wright
In Tobias Hochscherf and James Leggott (eds). *British Science Fiction Film and Television: Critical Essays* (Jefferson, NC: McFarland and Company, 2011), pp. 128–42.

Life in the Hiatus: New *Doctor Who* Fans, 1989–2005
Craig Owen Jones

'The Eighth is the first'
Margaret Brown
Whotopia 15 (November 2008), pp. 8–9

'The dispersible television text: Theorising moments of the new *Doctor Who*'
Matt Hills
In *Science Fiction Film and Television*. 1: 1 (2008), pp. 25–44.

Film/Television

Thirty Years In The TARDIS, Kevin Davies, creator (London, UK: BBC, 1993)
Noel's House Party, Noel Edmonds, creator (London, UK: BBC, 1991)
Eastenders, Julia Smith and Tony Holland, creators (London, UK: BBC, 1985)
Star Trek, Gene Roddenberry, creator (Hollywood, CA: CBS, 1966)
Doctor Who [Classic series], Sydney Newman and Verity Lambert, creators (London, UK: BBC, 1963); [New series], Russell T. Davies, creator (Cardiff, UK: BBC, 2005)

'The Name of the Doctor', Saul Metzstein, dir. *Doctor Who* [New series] (Cardiff, UK: BBC, 2013)
'The Eleventh Hour', Adam Smith, dir. *Doctor Who* [New series] (Cardiff, UK: BBC, 2010)
'The Next Doctor', Andy Goddard, dir. *Doctor Who* [New series] (Cardiff, UK: BBC, 2008)
Scream of the Shalka, Wilson Milam, dir. *Doctor Who* [Classic series] (London, UK: BBC, 2003)
Doctor Who: The Movie, Geoffrey Sax, dir. *Doctor Who* [Classic series] (Hollywood, CA: Fox and London, UK: BBC, 1996)
Dimensions In Time, Stuart MacDonald, dir. *Doctor Who* [Classic series] (London, UK: BBC, 1993)
Earthshock, Peter Grimwade, dir. *Doctor Who* [Classic series] (London, UK: BBC, 1982).
The Three Doctors, Lennie Mayne, dir. *Doctor Who* [Classic series] (London, UK: BBC, 1973)

ONE MAN'S LAW IS ANOTHER MAN'S CRIME. SLEEP ON IT, CHESTERTON. SLEEP ON IT.

THE 1ST DOCTOR
THE EDGE OF DESTRUCTION

Chapter
04

Britain as Fantasy: New Series *Doctor Who* in Young American Nerd Culture

Dylan Morris

→ Since its debut in the United Kingdom in 2005, New *Who* has acquired a sizeable fan base across the Atlantic in the United States. One core group within this American fan base are what I term proud 'young nerds' in their late teens and early twenties. These 'young nerds' are academically inclined young Americans with a passion for imaginative literature. They are well aware that fanatical enthusiasm for science fiction and fantasy can be seen as uncool or associated with social ineptitude, but they remain passionate about it.

Fig. 1: The 2011 Doctor Who Christmas Special, 'The Doctor, the Widow and the Wardrobe', paid homage to C.S. Lewis's Chronicles of Narnia and noted the similarity between the TARDIS and Lewis's titular Wardrobe. (Doctor Who ©BBC)

They aim to bring a self-aware, urbane and intellectual perspective to bear on the show, but they will also admit to loving it for its silliness. They are the fans likely to discuss uses of visual metaphor in 'Blink' (MacDonald, 2007, Series 3, Episode 10) or to write chapters like this one. In all this, they are not unlike proudly nerdy fans in *Doctor Who*'s homeland.

To see what might be more distinctive to the American fascination, I surveyed via e-mail 'young nerd' fans of New *Who* from both sides of the Atlantic. I used a snowball method; initial respondents forwarded the survey on to friends and fellow fans and also to university science fiction and fantasy societies, generating more responses. I also spoke in person to proudly nerdy fans of the show.

Every American young nerd I surveyed grew up reading the classics of British children's fantasy: works by Lewis Carroll, C. S. Lewis and J. R. R. Tolkien. These fans grew up with J. K. Rowling's *Harry Potter* (1997–2007). A vision of the British Isles as a land of whimsy and fantasy shapes their passion for *Doctor Who*. The show is a classic children's fantasy story that employs technology as its magic. Like Lewis's Lucy, Carroll's Alice and Rowling's Harry, the Doctor's companions are plucked from their prosaic lives into an exciting new world of fantastical adventure. The TARDIS, as the 2011 *Doctor Who* Christmas Special ('The Doctor, the Widow and the Wardrobe', Blackburn) pointed out, is the Wardrobe (Figure 1).

America is a country without a (fantastical) medieval European past. There are no castles, no stories of American knights, kings and queens. Young American nerds appropriate Britain as a second heritage that offers stronger mythic and magical possibilities. From prosaic America, they step through the doors of the TARDIS into a fantastical imagined Britain. This imagined Britain has more space for proud nerds and the whimsy they love than does America; the Doctor himself is a proud and eccentric nerd.

Nerds, geeks and fans

But what is a nerd? I asked my interviewees whether they considered themselves nerdy, geeky or both, and whether they saw a distinction between the two terms. Will, a 23-year-old American fan with a degree in history, gave a response typical of American proud nerd culture:

I would consider myself 'nerdy' – I define 'nerdy' as smart, intellectually engaged and curious, enthusiastic, and unafraid of unironically being a fan of something which the general population is either indifferent to or skeptical of. I define 'geeky' as leaning more toward the science/math/tech end of the spectrum, perhaps more intensely fo-

Britain as Fantasy:
New Series *Doctor Who* in Young American Nerd Culture
Dylan Morris

cused on one field, and more strongly self-defining as part of a community of geeks in opposition to the mainstream.

Will has appropriated and transformed the term 'nerd', originally derogatory school-yard slang for an intelligent, studious child. He takes pride in precisely those qualities that make very young nerds into targets for bullies and candidates for social ostracism: intelligence, curiosity and a willingness to express genuine, 'unironi[c]' enthusiasm for uncool cultural institutions (or a willingness to express 'too much' enthusiasm for cultural institutions that are socially acceptable to like, but not to love). Will does distinguish himself from the 'geek': the archetype of a socially awkward and often socially isolated 'math and science person'.

The United Kingdom is also home to proud nerds. David, a 20-year-old English university student, told me:

If one is going to pigeonhole people then there are two distinct types of people to pigeonhole, and I am one of them. I would be more likely to describe myself as "nerd" than anything else; I think "geek" carries a connotation of compsci [computer science]-ish-ness, whereas I just enjoy long, convoluted boardgames, fantasy, and science fiction and have a good memory for useless trivia.

King's College, Cambridge is presently home to a 'King's Nerdy Fangirl Society'. As of November 2012, the description of the Society on its official Facebook page reads as follows: 'Calling all self-defining fangirls! (*disclaimer* non-gender specific. Also, no twi-hards allowed :p) We love things. All of the things. Below are some examples of those things. If you love these things too, or similar things, Allons-y'. As 'Allons-y' – a reference to the Tenth Doctor's catchphrase – suggests, the nerdy fangirls of King's College love *Doctor Who*. They also love *The Lord of the Rings* (Tolkien books published 1954/1955; Jackson films released 2001–03), *Sherlock* (Moffat and Gatiss, BBC, 2010–present), and a number of other nerd- and fan-beloved fantasy and science fiction series. The fangirl is defined not by the specific sci-fi and fantasy cultural icons she adores, but rather by her unhidden adoration for a whole class of uncool things.

All American respondents who answered my question about nerds and geeks identified themselves as one of the two. Yet such slang is fluid. While I use 'young nerd' as a term of art in this chapter, I do not mean to imply that the way in which I use it is the single proper meaning of 'nerd'. Nor do I mean to imply that all young American nerds are *Doctor Who* fans, or that all American Whovians are young nerds. I use the term 'young nerd' precisely to make clear that I am examining a particular subgroup within the *Who* fan base. I also do not argue that every young and nerdy American *Doctor Who* fan imagines Britain in the ways I describe here; I rather aim to illustrate one telling way in which some of these fans relate to New *Who*.

These young nerds are distinguished from *Doctor Who* fans in general by several characteristics. They are young adults who typically have come to the New series in young adulthood; they are neither the children who make up the show's official target audience nor the slightly older fans who remember Classic *Who*. In watching *Doctor Who*, they display their relatively unabashed love of things that it may not be cool for people their age to adore. They tend to be academically inclined, and they use their intelligence to analyse the show in both serious and silly ways.

Britain as homeland: Appropriating a medieval past for America

American nerds, with their unabashed love of imaginative literature, are predisposed to like *Doctor Who*, just as the Nerdy Fangirls at King's College, Cambridge do. But for Americans like Will, *Doctor Who* fandom can be about more than nerdiness:

My senior year in college, more and more of my intellectual-nerdy friends were vocally enthusing about *Doctor Who*. I felt increasingly out of the loop, and feared that in order to maintain my status as an up-to-date nerd and Anglophile I would need to cave and check it out.

Will does not simply care about being an 'up-to-date nerd'; he also wants to be an 'up-to-date … Anglophile'.

British fans I interviewed for this chapter do believe that *Doctor Who* is recognizably and even emblematically British. Viola, a 19-year-old British student, pointed out that the show is itself as much 'a part of our [British] culture' as British culture is a part of *Doctor Who*. Yet for her, *Doctor Who*'s ultimate appeal is cross-cultural: 'the fundamentally appealing aspects of the show – the characters, relationships and central concept – don't rely on cultural references; they are universal. The cultural references are arguably a bonus for the UK viewers'.

What Viola might be surprised to hear is that these references are a bonus for some American viewers as well. Paula, a 22-year-old American graduate student, told me:

Part of the reason I love *Doctor Who* (and other shows of similar caliber) is because it's incredibly British. British television has a different ethos when it comes to what makes a show interesting – instead of explosions [...] it depends on subtle social commentary and men in wigs.

Will agrees:

[Watching *Doctor Who*] makes me feel more connected to British culture, and also part of an Anglophilic American cognoscenti, and somehow it also softens and humanizes the often-imposing British cultural edifice to know that the nation is in thrall to such a

Britain as Fantasy:
New Series *Doctor Who* in Young American Nerd Culture
Dylan Morris

wonderful but fundamentally silly show.

Will called himself 'highly Anglophilic'. Similarly, asked if she considered herself an Anglophile, Grace, a 24-year-old United States Air Force officer stationed in the United Kingdom said: 'I adore all aspects of Great Britain and Northern Ireland.' Whether Anglophiles like Will or more general 'Britophiles' like Grace, these young nerds feel a cultural attachment to the British Isles. Many adore a very specific Britain: the Britain of British children's fantasy. As noted, they read Lewis and Tolkien, among others, and grew up with Rowling's Harry. Yet many of them also read and loved classic children's fantasy by Americans: *The Wizard of Oz* (Baum, 1900); *A Wrinkle in Time* (L'Engle 1962). Why be a Britophile?

The British past strikes numerous Americans, nerdy or otherwise, as having better mythical and fantastical possibilities than America's own. John, a 23-year-old law student and nerdy fan, contended that 'there is a mystique about the British countryside that America lacks'. His view is not uncommon among Americans. Journalist Brian Wheeler has pointed out that actors in American fantasy films and television series tend to speak with British accents. Some American fantasy authors have deliberately worked with British motifs: Lloyd Alexander's *Chronicles of Prydain* (1964–1968) are set in a Wales-like fantasy nation; George R. R. Martin's *A Song of Ice and Fire* (1996–present) draws liberally upon the War of the Roses for inspiration.

Why might this be? Scott, a 24-year-old student and nerdy *Doctor Who* fan who loves Lewis and Tolkien, spoke of

Britain's linguistic and ethnic diversity, ancient monuments, pagan beliefs and overall long history – all of which have been appropriated as 'British' in some way and viewed as the nation's heritage, unlike America, where our ancient past is Other: Native American.

Scott points out the sensitive issues of ethnicity and nationalism that underlie this American idea of fantasy. Fantasy, for many non-Native Americans, has a distinctly medieval European twinge. They look to Europe, not to America's indigenous peoples. They take Britain's past – and hence its mythology – as their birthright. There have been attempts to write an American children's fantasy that draws upon Native American mythologies, but the more 'classic' image of fantasy involves distinctly European knights, castles and wizards. For those who celebrate a more multicultural America, this can be troubling: American fantasy author Ursula LeGuin deliberately described Ged, her eponymous *Wizard of Earthsea* (1968), as dark-skinned. Recent editions of the book sport covers that depict him as white.

American visions of fantastical Britain reflect discomfiting truths about ethnicity and power in the United States, but they do also help explain why an American fantasy fans' attachment to British culture. For some Americans, to love fantasy and to love Britain are then nearly the same thing.

Britain as fantasy land: The Atlantic as a rabbit-hole

Most British children's fantasy is not 'high fantasy' set in a wholly parallel (if medieval Europe-inspired) universe. Rather, it is what I term 'rabbit-hole' fantasy. The hero or heroine, always a child, lives a prosaic life in a modern real world, but escapes through some portal into a magical world that exists next to or within the 'real world': a Wonderland, a Narnia, a Hogwarts. Many in the real world – most notably adults – do not notice or ignore the fantastical realities that brush up against them. The only adults who tend to notice the fantastical and admit its existence are wise grandparent-figures who have regained or who never lost their capacity for wonder.

As I have suggested above, New *Who* is a rabbit-hole fantasy. The companion, as much an audience avatar as is a Pevensie child, steps through a magic portal into a still more magical world. He or (more often) she often has an initially oblivious parent-figure, or, in the case of Donna Noble, a less skeptical grandparent. Often ignored or unappreciated in the real world, the companion discovers that she has a special and important role to play in the magical world. Rose Tyler, Martha Jones, Donna Noble and Amy Pond have all saved the Earth. Some have saved the entire universe.

Precisely where is the boundary between the magical and prosaic worlds in a British rabbit-hole fantasy? The answer may be different for Americans than it is for Brits. For British readers, *Harry Potter* took a familiar cultural institution – the English boarding school – and made it fantastical. American readers have reacted differently. At Yale in the mid-2000s, hundreds of students joined a Facebook group entitled 'I chose Yale because it's like Hogwarts', a reference to Yale's gothic architecture. Reacting in a similar way to a different series, Yale graduate Will has made pilgrimages to Oxford to seek out locations described in Pullman's *His Dark Materials* (1995–2000).

To these Americans (and, perhaps, to Brits not from the Eton-Oxbridge set), the English boarding school and the British university are themselves part of the fantasy story's unfamiliar alternate world. For them, Britain means fantasy not only because it means the mythical version of the Self – one's own past but with knights and castles – but equally because it means a fantastical Other – a fantastical land on the other side of an Atlantic rabbit-hole.

Some American fans discover that the other side of this rabbit-hole feels much more like home than their real-world residence; they identify with the aspects of *Doctor Who* that they see as quintessentially British. Tricia, a 25-year-old United States Air Force officer stationed in the United Kingdom, explained:

[*Doctor Who*] actually didn't strike me as particularly British until I'd lived in the UK. I think it's because I grew up reading so many of the right kind of books. And I naturally have more of a wry, sharp type [of] humor. I just thought I wasn't funny, or that other

Britain as Fantasy:
New Series *Doctor Who* in Young American Nerd Culture
Dylan Morris

Fig. 2: Doctor Who in the Wild West: A rabbit-hole fantasy for Brits? (Doctor Who ©BBC)

people didn't get it, and I didn't know why [until going to Britain].

She added:

My parents always told me I would fit in in English culture, but maybe more the school type English culture. I was one of those American kids who wanted to go to Oxford. I like tweed and boots. And elbow patches. And jackets and scarves. I know that's kind of stereotypical, but it's also kind of true.

Tricia feels at home in the tweedy version of Britain that New *Who* often celebrates, thanks to having read 'the right kind of books' – British children's fantasy novels – as a child. Now a young woman, she has happily travelled down the rabbit-hole.

When the BBC announced that the opening episodes of Series 6 would be set in the United States, some Brits speculated that this might be an effort to appeal to Yanks, but *Doctor Who* showrunner Steven Moffat understands his American fans. He told *The Guardian* in 2011: 'We just had a story that got us excited, and America was the natural setting. Truth is, an American setting isn't necessarily the way to an American audience's hearts, because it's not exactly something they're starved of.'

If anything, Moffat's American settings might be seen as an attempt to satisfy *British* desires for rabbit-hole fantasy. Most Moffat-era American episodes have taken place at least partially in the American West (Figure 2). The Wild West is an American romanticized past, with cowboys in place of knights. Perhaps the American West is alluring to Moffat in the way that Britain is alluring to young American nerds – as the other side of a rabbit-hole. Yet there is little chance that *Doctor Who* will cease to be 'British' in the eyes of young American nerds. *Doctor Who*'s writers treasure a similar imagined Britain.

British fantasies: The Doctor as nerd-hero and Brit-hero

If young, nerdy American *Doctor Who* fans are in love with a particular imagined Britain, it is in part because the show itself promotes a similar vision of the nation. Cooper, a 23-year-old American editorial assistant and *Doctor Who* fan, argued that the show valorizes a 'specifically professorial, silly, tweedy, plucky, stiff-upper-lippy kind of Britishness. [...] the messages often seem ideal-Britain ones of fair play, silliness and being the little island using cleverness, pluck and compassion against huge, calculating, cold, amoral, totalitarian (fascist) enemies'.

This mythological British self-conception is not unlike the self-conception of the proud nerd. 'Yes,' say Brits, 'we're odd ducks. But we're also smarter and more self-aware than the less whimsical nationals of other countries.' Cooper mentioned the World Wars, but such thinking also extends to Britain's much friendlier transatlantic rivalry with America. Brits often claim that most Americans 'don't get' British humour, and there is more than a hint of pride in that statement. Americans are too prosaic. 'We,' Brits of certain stripes tell themselves, 'are wittier and more sophisticated.' American proud nerds tell themselves a similar self-validating story about their relationship to a mainstream American culture that does not always value them. They, too, are wittier and more sophisticated. Tricia's proud claim to have a British sense of humour is as characteristic of a certain kind of young nerd as it is of a certain kind of British patriot.

Britain, a former imperial power, can no longer claim to 'rule the waves'. Instead, it declares itself the land of wit and wry self-awareness and mocks American blunt, literal speech and brute force. The ex-empire thinks of itself as the underdog. 'Superpower' America is the land of bellicose bluster. Proud nerds similarly recognize that mainstream social power typically belongs to more conventional young adults. Their response is like that of the Brits; if they cannot be superior in might, they can be superior in sophistication.

Even as she serves in the American military, Tricia distinguishes herself from unsophisticated American jokesters and allies herself instead with Brits and their 'wry, sharp' humour. The irony is that this behaviour can fuel the very same British snobbery towards America with which Tricia associates herself. Reading British studies of American Anglophilia such as Christopher Hitchens's 1990 *Blood, Class and Nostalgia*, one sometimes catches a hint of disdain: American aspiration to imagined English refinement only serves to prove that Americans are rubes.

Still, nerdy American *Doctor Who* fans like Tricia embrace this English and British nationalist mythology. They imagine Britain as a land with more space for the life of the mind than America offers, a better place to be a nerd. *Doctor Who*'s British writers enable this; they conceive of and portray their homeland in precisely these terms.

The Doctor himself embodies the show's celebration of British whimsy, wit and intellect. Particularly in the New series, he triumphs through brains – through quick thinking and quicker talking – rather than through brawn. At first blush, this might seem more sci-fi than fantasy, more geek than nerd. *Doctor Who* is not 'hard' science fiction, though. Rather, like fantasy, *Doctor Who* emphasizes the power of words, writing and speech. From Tolkien's wicked Saruman with his subtle rhetoric to Rowling's benevolent Dumbledore with his pseudo-Latin incantations, the wizards of fantasy command using language.

The Doctor is more wizard than scientist. His power also comes from speech. One of his most iconic traits is his liberal use of technobabble. 'Reverse the polarity of the neutron flow' is a Third Doctor original, and the various Doctors since have continued the tradition of using unexplained science-y sounding blather to get out of scrapes. The Doctor's technobabble is nerdy wordplay, not geeky 'compsci-ish-ness'. There is no scientific content. Technobabble instead showcases the Doctor's ability to think on his feet and demonstrates his capacity for verbal wit and humour. The Doctor is at his most vulnerable when his verbal gifts desert him or are stolen from him; the episode

Britain as Fantasy:
New Series *Doctor Who* in Young American Nerd Culture
Dylan Morris

'Midnight' (Troughton, 2008, Series 4, Episode 8) turns precisely upon this point. Will, an avowed inveterate lover of puns and word games, has fallen particularly in love with Matt Smith's Eleventh Doctor, who babbles at a rate that makes his New series predecessors seem taciturn.

Smith has played the Doctor-as-nerd to the hilt. His Doctor is socially awkward, but proudly so. Some of Eleven's awkwardness – giving Amy and Rory a bunk-bed instead of a double bed – seems puckishly calculated. Smith's Doctor adores wordplay and exults in his own verbal gymnastics. Above all, he is an inveterate and proud lover of the uncool: 'bowties are cool,' he declares, not caring, or perhaps even proud, that those around him disagree.

Most of all, like the American young nerd, the Eleventh Doctor is proudly on the side of children in the war of child against parent, wonder against cynicism and magical against 'real' world that animates rabbit-hole fantasy. He refuses to sacrifice his unjaded love of uncool things – not least fantastical stories. So strong is this trait that when the Doctor does turn world-weary and cynical, as he does at points in Series 7, we are meant to understand by this that he is suffering emotionally and psychologically. A healthily un-cynical Doctor would doubtless agree with C. S. Lewis, who wrote:

When I was ten, I read fairy tales in secret and would have been ashamed if I had been found doing so. Now that I am fifty I read them openly. When I became a man I put away childish things, including the fear of childishness and the desire to be very grown up.

The 50-year-old Lewis and the many-hundreds-of-years-old Doctor are kindred spirits; 'There's no point in being grown up if you can't act a little childish sometimes,' the Fourth Doctor declares in the serial *Robot* (Barry, 1974–75, Season 12).

Conclusion: A children's show?
Proud nerds enter the world of *Doctor Who* without fear of childishness. Rabbit-hole fantasy plays upon the powerful longings that a child feels: to be special when the world makes her feel unimportant, to be powerful when the world makes him feel weak, to be appreciated when the world makes her feel ignored. A fantastical, imagined Britain with more space for the life of the mind and for the unabashed love of uncool things – a Britain in which the Doctor can be cool – entices the American young nerd down the rabbit-hole.

Is this a naive aspirational fantasy, an easy target for the mocking pen of a British cultural critic? Here, perhaps, C. S. Lewis and the Doctor have a point. Imagining a Britain with elements of whimsy and fantasy need not mean idealizing Britain. To assume so is to assume that wonder requires obliviousness and *naïveté*. Such a belief is itself naive. To be analytical is not to be dispassionate. One can feel the persuasive force of a myth and delight in being partially persuaded even if one understands the ways in which that myth is false. That is the delight of reading or watching good fantasy. 'Fundamentally silly' though he may declare the show to be, Will enjoys allowing himself be persuaded by *Doctor Who*'s rhetoric of whimsy. Along with other young and nerdy American *Doctor Who* fans, he takes pleasure in letting himself believe at least a little in the fantastical place that is the Doctor's Britain. ●

GO FURTHER

Books

The Humanism of Doctor Who: *A Critical Study in Science Fiction and Philosophy*
David Layton
(Jefferson, NC: McFarland, 2012)

Accent on Privilege: English Identities and Anglophilia in the U.S.
Katharine W. Jones
(Philadelphia: Temple University Press, 2001)

Blood, Class and Nostalgia: Anglo-American Ironies
Christopher Hitchens
(New York: Farrar, Strauss and Giroux, 1990)

Extracts/Essays/Articles

'On three ways of writing for children'
C. S. Lewis
In *Of Other Worlds: Essays and Stories* (Boston, MA: Houghton Mifflin Harcourt, 2002), pp. 22–34.

Film/Television

Sherlock, Steven Moffat and Mark Gatiss, creators (Cardiff, UK: BBC, 2010)
Doctor Who [Classic series], Sydney Newman and Verity Lambert, creators (London, UK: BBC, 1963); [New series], Russell T. Davies, creator (Cardiff, UK: BBC, 2005)

'The Doctor, the Widow and the Wardrobe', Farren Blackburn, dir. *Doctor Who* (Cardiff, UK: BBC, 2011)
'Midnight', Alice Troughton, dir. *Doctor Who* [New series] (Cardiff, UK: BBC, 2008)
'Blink' Hettie MacDonald, dir. *Doctor Who* [New series] (Cardiff, UK: BBC, 2007)

Britain as Fantasy:
New Series *Doctor Who* in Young American Nerd Culture
Dylan Morris

Robot, Christopher Barry, dir. *Doctor Who* [Classic series] (London, UK: BBC, 1974–75)

Online
Extracts/Essays/Articles

'Why are fantasy world accents British?'
Brian Wheeler
BBC News Magazine. 30 March 2012, http://www.bbc.co.uk/news/magazine-17554816

'*Doctor Who* takes Tardis to US'
Vicky Frost
The Guardian. 22 April 2011, http://www.guardian.co.uk/tv-and-radio/2011/apr/22/doctor-who-tardis-in-us

'There'll always be an England: Anglophilia as antimodern leisure'
Michael Plato
In *College Quarterly*. 13: 4 (2010), http://www.collegequarterly.ca/2010-vol13-num04-fall/plato.html.

'Spectrums of investment in *Doctor Who* fandom' [Thesis]
Stephen J. Duckworth
Brunel University, 2006, http://bura.brunel.ac.uk/handle/2438/5341

'Do the Americans get irony?'
Jonathan Duffy
BBC News Online. 27 January 2004, http://news.bbc.co.uk/1/hi/magazine/3433375.stm

'A quiet joke at your expense'
The Economist. 18 December 1999, http://www.economist.com/node/268955

Websites

'King's Nerdy Fangirl Society', http://www.facebook.com/groups/114195412068662

FIVE MILLION CYBERMEN, EASY. ONE DOCTOR, NOW YOU'RE SCARED.

ROSE
ARMY OF GHOSTS / DOOMSDAY

Chapter 05

'You Anorak': The *Doctor Who* Experience and Experiencing *Doctor Who*

Teresa Forde

→ Fandom in the Whoniverse can be understood as a series of participations, negotiations and engagements with *Doctor Who* as a popular cultural phenomenon. This chapter will explore the *Doctor Who* Experience, a themed visitor centre in Cardiff Bay, and consider the relationship between the academic and fan as consumer, fan participation, immersion and interactivity, and the relationship between fandom and consumption at the Experience.

Fig. 1: Daleks on Display. (Doctor Who ©BBC Worldwide)

Due to the longevity of *Doctor Who*, there are increasing ways to access and consume aspects of the Whoniverse. For example, my experience of watching *Doctor Who* as a child is markedly different to my children's interaction with the series. My initial memories of *Doctor Who* are of the Third Doctor (Jon Pertwee) with his companion Sarah Jane Smith (Elisabeth Sladen). Additional information about *Doctor Who* would come from *Look-in*, an ITV's children's television magazine (1971–94) or a special Christmas feature in the BBC's *Radio Times*. In contrast, contemporary access to multimedia platforms and games offers the potential to revisit any *Doctor Who* episode at any time and an array of opportunities to find out and share information about *Doctor Who*.

'You anorak!': Aca-fans and the academy

This account of *Doctor Who* fan phenomena is called 'You anorak' because this is the response I received when mentioning a planned visit to the *Doctor Who* Experience. The term 'anorak' is most often applied to a subject area that is not defined as traditionally academic and acknowledges the role of a fan who accumulates information, used in relation to trainspotters who would wear anoraks on early morning trips to train stations to record carriage numbers. The comment 'you anorak' may have also been made specifically about my intention to visit the *Doctor Who* Experience as it is a visit to a themed 'spin-off' of the Whoniverse and may hold additional connotations of commercialism similar to visiting a theme park based on fictional characters may be viewed differently to accessing a traditional archive of academic interest (Figure 1).

In order to account for fans' often alternative readings of popular cult texts, Henry Jenkins (1992) has referred to fans as textual poachers who illicitly construct resistant or 'unofficial' and sometimes explicit readings of characters through fanfiction. Jenkins considered the Kirk/Spock relationship in *Star Trek* (Roddenberry, CBS, 1966–69). Similar readings still proliferate in contemporary fan writing; for example, on Tumblr with the relationship between Amy Pond and the Doctor, as in the 'ship Amy/Doctor, or even the Doctor and Sherlock Holmes making the crossover relationship of *Wholock* (see Nistasha Perez's chapter in this volume). In a consideration of cult fandom, Matt Hills asks whether academics are themselves textual poachers, as readings of a text can be 'appropriated by its professional academic poachers', implying a clear relationship between fan and academic readings. Certainly academic writing might form playful alternative readings as well.

In an interview with Suzanne Scott, in the 2012 update of his work on *Textual Poachers*, Henry Jenkins uses the term aca-fan to describe the fan/academic identity. For

'You Anorak':
The *Doctor Who* Experience and Experiencing *Doctor Who*
Teresa Forde

Jenkins, part of the aca-fan's research is the need for personal reflection on being a fan of popular culture. Jenkins distinguishes between those who see themselves as individual fans and those immersed within a wider fan community. My position is a negotiation between an individual fan and a wider academic interest. Subjective experience accounts for the pleasure gained from popular culture texts and for an immersion in what Jenkins calls 'participatory culture'. I would argue that fan participation should be recognized as diverse and working on different levels to avoid exclusion. It could also be argued that the producer/fan embodies contemporary writers of *Doctor Who* who actively embrace their own forms of (boyhood) fandom, represented by Steven Moffat and Mark Gatiss. Attractions such as the *Doctor Who* Experience come in the wake of *Doctor Who* conventions that have become key events in their own right. As Mark Jancovich argues in relation to cult film, 'cult movie fandom emerged not as a reaction against the market or the academy, but rather through their historical development'. In this light, the relationship between fandom, television production and academic research appears to be distinctly complementary.

The *Doctor Who* Experience is a commercial venture from BBC Worldwide offering the opportunity for fans to engage with sets and props, and provides the possibility of fan immersion and interactivity in a multimedia museum environment. Although it is not a traditional museum, the *Doctor Who* Experience demonstrates the ways in which contemporary museums make themselves seemingly more interactive and accessible to the public. Its website describes access to 'the world's most extensive collection of original *Doctor Who* props and artefacts'. As Robert Lumley observes, 'Far from making museums obsolete, the media environment has had two main effects: first, to push museums to do what *only* they can do; second, to give rise to a new generation of multi-media museums.' The *Doctor Who* Experience appeals to a range of fans, from those who wear a long coat or a 'cool' bow tie to emulate the Tenth or Eleventh Doctor's costume during their visit, to visitors who might remember the older Doctors with as much fondness as their more recent incarnations. The heterogeneity of fandom complements the notion of 'participatory culture' as fan behaviour can be separated into different forms of participation rather than just the consideration of a 'typical' fan.

Flânerie, consumption and tourism: 'Bow ties, fezzes and Stetsons are cool'
The *Doctor Who* Experience has been relocated back in Cardiff Bay. It is situated not too far from BBC Wales and can be identified by the TARDIS blue that stands out against the skyline. One of the main draws of the *Doctor Who* Experience is the exhibition of original sets, costumes, and props including the Third Doctor's sporty yellow car, Bessie, and River Song's (Alex Kingston) diary displayed in the foyer. The museum includes Daleks and Cybermen and other aliens, outfits belonging to all the Doctors and some of their companions, as well as other props such as reproductions of Van Gogh paintings and various masks and animatronics. As representative of the world of *Doctor Who*, the

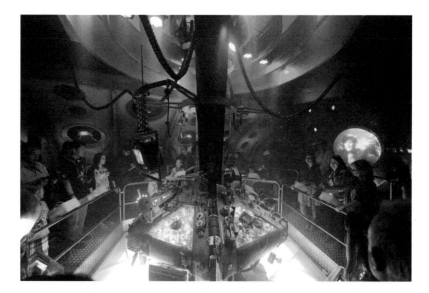

Experience also aims to encapsulate the spirit of the series. The first part of the Experience consists of a walk through section set up as an action sequence simulating part of a story of alien attack. The second part of the Experience is a museum displaying various costumes and props from the series.

Visitors to the *Doctor Who* Experience may be viewed as fans, consumers or tourists. Even for visitors who come from Cardiff, the *Doctor Who* Experience is a tourist destination and is clearly part of the tourist industry and the planned regeneration of Cardiff Bay. Visiting Cardiff becomes significant in recognizing the implication of BBC Cardiff's location shoots: when we visited we stayed in a street that had been used as a location for the episode 'Rise of the Cybermen' (Harper, 2006, Series 2, Episode 5). Of course, Cardiff has also been used to film the spin-off series *Torchwood* (Davies, BBC, 2006–11).

The interactive part of the *Doctor Who* Experience begins with a video of the Eleventh Doctor (Matt Smith) who addresses the visitors as shoppers, implying either that they have seemingly stumbled into the TARDIS unawares or perhaps are 'shopping' for an experience (Figure 2).

The idea of shoppers as cultural 'grazers' has its roots in Walter Benjamin's development in *The Arcades Project* (2002) of the *flâneur* who saunters through the city, surveying all there is to see. But the 'shoppers' who visit the Experience are not deemed to be idly strolling so much as carrying bags and consuming: these are modern day shoppers for whom it is a leisure activity to buy.

Developing the active connotation of the *flâneur* or shopper, Rob Shields recognizes the *flâneur* as a consumer of capitalism and culture who signified a shift within economic and social changes as well as changes in 'social spatialization', particularly in the nineteenth century which is encapsulated in the Victorian period often returned to within the episodes of New *Who*. In Shields's view, the *flâneur* may feel unsettled yet excited by the ability to travel to more of the world through the development of transport and commerce. This expanding and developing world was to be marvelled and experienced. To Shield, '*Flânerie* is the psychotic appropriation of space and time. On

'You Anorak':
The *Doctor Who* Experience and Experiencing *Doctor Who*
Teresa Forde

the one hand, the city was explored and visually consumed as a series of "exotic" sights; on the other hand, the *flâneur* consumed time, measured in terms of bodily footsteps and consumption'. *Flânerie* involves the experiences of watching and buying, wandering and consuming.

Within the *Doctor Who* Experience visitors are initially identified as shoppers who have wandered into the place. They then become part of an adventure as they are 'chased' by the Daleks and jostled by the TARDIS in a scenario familiar to many of the Doctor's companions in the series. The visitors/shoppers to the Experience are playing the part of companions and are also potentially at the mercy of the Dalek foe. The idea that we are shoppers, haphazardly being drawn into this adventure, is also amusing as we have to just get on with everything in a similar way to the Doctor's companions must get involved when they first meet him. After all, Rose Tyler (Billie Piper) worked in a shop before she met the Ninth Doctor. Perhaps the Doctor is the ultimate *flâneur*, perusing the world in his TARDIS as he passes by. But despite roaming across the universe, the Doctor does immerse himself in Earth's concerns, is often accused of creating its problems, and has a heart (or two).

We are also shoppers in buying into the Experience and encountering the inevitable exit through the gift shop. Although one may not 'buy into' all the merchandizing and paraphernalia that can accompany fan interest, fans may wish to buy objects that conjure up a sense of the Whoniverse. The item obtained from the gift shop is a memento and can become memory work in itself. As Kuhn suggests, 'perhaps the archetypal memory object is the souvenir' which becomes 'a token of remembrance', a 'keepsake'. In the context of *Doctor Who* merchandise the purchase takes on an additional significance in commemorating the visit as an experience.

Fans can engage with favoured texts and objects for their use value rather than their exchange value. The exchange value of an item is its monetary value and the use value is the value to its owner, or its purpose. The use value accounts for pleasure and for entertainment, but the value of the products and their rarity may also be significant to a collector. Use value can be split between actual use, such as the practical purpose of an item such as a mug, and symbolic value, which accounts for the additional meaning in owning a *Doctor Who* mug. Suzan Boztepe recognizes in the context of design that objects can embody often very personalized meanings for their owners as 'they often value objects not for what they do, or what they are made of, but for what they signify'. The merchandise can become both a very personal possession and a way of sharing memories and emotions. The use or symbolic value of *Doctor Who* merchandizing is significant, as the objects are part of an extended world of *Doctor Who*. In our exit through the gift shop we did come away with a facsimile TARDIS door and a poster delineating that 'Everything I need to know I learned from *Doctor Who*' including a number of the caveats, two of which have been used in subheadings within this chapter.

I would add that even a themed object or purchase comes to represent something temporally specific: time spent with someone at the *Doctor Who* Experience; the memory of watching a favourite episode or Doctor; pleasure in (shared) rereadings or interpretations. The fan as consumer can also influence the production of *Doctor Who* in a form of 'co-creation' which, for Prahalad and Ramaswamy, involves 'creating an experience environment in which consumers can have active dialogue and co-construct personalized experiences' so even with the same product 'customers can construct different experiences' whether shared or personal.

The notion of fans being potential co-creators of *Doctor Who* relates directly to the consumerist element of fandom. It is clear that such co-creation involves the intention of a personalizing effect on the part of the user or consumer. Co-creation implies but does not necessarily mean co-production in its traditional sense but may often describe a dialogue between producer and consumer and allows space to develop alternative meanings. As Sue Short recognizes in her consideration of the 2011 *Cult Telefantasy Series*, the fan can fulfil the role of the perfect consumer-viewer, providing audience feedback as each episode airs. An example of the direct fan-as-consumer influence promoted at the *Doctor Who* Experience is the *Doctor Who* Consumer Panel, which is run by BBC Worldwide and has a waiting list of fans keen to provide feedback. Equally, the television series may occasionally respond to fan pressure as seen in the episode 'The Angels Take Manhattan' (Hurran, 2012, Series 7, Episode 5). The loss of Rory and Amy from the Eleventh Doctor's world was greeted with much concern by fans who wanted to see what had happened to Brian, Rory's dad. This fan response led to the decision to post online an animated storyboard of the unmade sequence, '*Doctor Who: P.S.*' (2012) by Chris Chibnall, which shows Rory's dad reading his son's letter and acts as a significant point of closure for fans. The *Doctor Who* Experience acts as a contemporary media experience and seeks feedback from visitors in relation to specific fan based views and opinions.

Playing games in the Whoniverse: 'Football's the one with the sticks, isn't it?'
The *Doctor Who* Experience offers the opportunity to play in the Whoniverse. As the website explains:

Step through a crack in time and help the Doctor, armed with his Sonic Screwdriver to escape from his foes, fly the TARDIS and come face-to-face with some of the scariest monsters seen on screen. Featuring exclusive filmed sequences with Matt Smith and packed with amazing special effects this multi-sensory experience is fun for the family and fans alike.

Although acknowledging all the Doctors, the videos running in the Experience feature the Tenth and Eleventh Doctors, David Tennant and Matt Smith. A review from a contributor to *Den of Geek!* enthuses about the Experience in its former temporary

'You Anorak':
The *Doctor Who* Experience and Experiencing *Doctor Who*
Teresa Forde

home at the London Olympia: 'I'll tell you why the Doctor Who Experience is genius. It's because it really gets fandom.' The review recognizes the interest in and identification with the Doctor's companions: 'Especially since 2005, the companion role in Doctor Who has paralleled that of us fans, intrigued, surprised, sometimes annoyed and a little bit obsessed with the Doctor.' So the personal and intimate relationships between the Doctor and his companions provide an important mechanism of engagement with the newest Doctors in particular.

As part of this engagement, the Experience offers the possibility of immersion and interactivity, terms often used to describe a player's relationship to computer games and multimedia platforms. Within computer game play the avatar represents the player's presence on screen. Playability and control are significant factors, with agency being a key consideration in game play. Sue Morris makes a distinction between playing first-person shooter games and watching cinema. In game-playing time is real but warped, the player enters into the space of the game and the player is highly involved; in cinema time is edited, viewers are absorbed in the film gaze and are less highly involved. Both of these forms of interaction are relevant to the Experience.

In game-playing, the agency of the player's avatar, the ability to make things happen, is highly valued. Michael Mateas and Andrew Stern champion emergent narratives as spaces for player agency and influence, 'providing a rich framework within which individual players can construct their own narratives, or groups of players can engage in the shared social construction of narratives'. However, they question the lack of empowerment in games where players undertake the pretence of pressing buttons and pulling levers: 'If there are many buttons and knobs for the player to twiddle, but all the twiddling has little effect on experience, there is no agency.' Of course, a quintessential aspect of the *Doctor Who* series involves pressing buttons and pulling levers whilst standing in front of the TARDIS engine pretending to be jostled or thrown around. So when visitors to the *Doctor Who* Experience pretend to pull levers to engage the TARDIS they can both be immersed in the simulation of being in the TARDIS and have a taste of what the cast of the series experiences (Figure 3).

As Annette Kuhn argues, 'Performances of memory, moreover, can be – and are – enacted across a range of activities, places, rituals and media.' Kuhn emphasizes the ways in which we can use visual media as a vehicle to access memories and experiences. Even the act of looking can be a shared and social experience. In the display section, one of the more poignant moments of the series, the Tenth Doctor's (David Tennant) departure before regeneration as he declares 'I don't want to go!', is replayed on a video loop in front of a TARDIS for people to watch so they share in the replay of this memorable and emotive sequence over and over again. The video is played in front of a TARDIS engine for visitors to stand around whilst watching the Doctor's 'demise'. In considering the behaviour of tourists, John Urry proposes that the tourist gaze is performed as part of a social experience: 'Gazing almost always involves significant others. Gazing is an interactive, communal game where individual gazes are mediated and affected by the presence and gazes of others.' Existing in a public space, the *Doctor Who* Experience enables interaction and negotiation of groups of fans and visitors within the participatory culture of *Doctor Who* fandom. The act of 'negotiated gazing', and one could add listening, in itself remains a crucial and active performative strategy within the *Doctor Who* Experience.

Fantasy heritage: 'We're all stories in the end. Just make it a good one'
In order to understand the role of fantasy within spaces such as the *Doctor Who* Experience it is useful to consider Bærenholdt and Haldrup's account of the ways in which visitors to *Viking Ship Museum* perform ludic, or game-playing, activities: 'fantasy and realism are intertwined, especially when the imagination emerges from a series of bodily encounters – many but short – with "real" objects that are no more "real" than the products of fantasy'.

As part of the tour of the museum, Bærenholdt and Haldrup describe the way in which tourists 'perform heritage'. Through a negotiation between history and story, visitors to the Viking Ship Museum experience a 'fantastic realism'. The history of the Vikings becomes intertwined with objects and encounters designed to simulate visitors as they move around the museum. As part of the world of science fiction and telefantasy the *Doctor Who* Experience forms part of a much larger archive of television history open to visitors to be players, shoppers, consumers and fans. Perhaps, instead of negotiating the 'real', what visitors to the *Doctor Who* Experience can do is perform 'fantasy heritage'. Fans can don their anoraks, or more precisely bow ties and fezzes, and perform an engagement with the fantasy heritage in the world of *Doctor Who*. ●

GO FURTHER

Books

The Tourist Gaze 3.0
John Urry and Jonas Larsen
(London: Sage, 2011)

Cult Telefantasy Series: A Critical Analysis of The Prisoner, Twin Peaks, The X-Files, Buffy the Vampire Slayer, Lost, Heroes, Doctor Who *and* Star Trek
Sue Short
(Jefferson, NC: McFarland, 2011)

'You Anorak':
The *Doctor Who* Experience and Experiencing *Doctor Who*
Teresa Forde

The Arcades Project
Walter Benjamin (trans. Howard Eiland and Kevin McLaughlin)
(Cambridge: Harvard University Press, 2002)

Textual Poachers: Television Fans and Participatory Culture
Henry Jenkins
(New York: Routledge, 1992)

Extracts/Essays/Articles

'Textual poachers: Twenty years later: A conversation between Henry Jenkins and Suzanne Scott'
Henry Jenkins
In *Textual Poachers: Television Fans and Participatory Culture* (London: Routledge, 2012), pp. vii–l.

'Memory texts and memory work: Performances of memory in and with visual media'
Annette Kuhn
In *Memory Studies*. 3: 4 (2010), pp. 293–97.

'User value: Competing theories and models'
Suzan Boztepe
In *International Journal of Design*. 1: 2 (2007), pp. 52–63.

'Interaction and narrative'
Michael Mateas and Andrew Stern
In John Benjamins (ed). *The Game Design Reader: A Rules of Play Anthology* (Cambridge: MIT Press, 2006), pp. 642–669.

'Academic textual poachers: *Blade Runner* as cult canonical movie'
Matt Hills
In Will Brooker (ed). *The Blade Runner Experience: The Legend of a Science Fiction Classic* (London: Wallflower, 2005), pp. 124–41.

'On the track of the Vikings'
Jorgen Ole Bærenholdt and Michael Haldrup
In Mimi Sheller and John Urry (eds). *Tourism Mobilities: Places to Play, Places in Play* (London: Routledge, 2004), pp. 78–89.

'Co-creation experiences: The next practice in value creation'
C. K. Prahalad and Venkat Ramaswamy
In *Journal of Interactive Marketing*. 18: 3 (2004), pp. 5–14.

'Cult fictions: Cult movies, subcultural capital and the production of cultural distinctions'
Mark Jancovich
In *Cultural Studies*. 16: 2 (2002), pp. 306–22.

'First-person shooters: A game apparatus'
Sue Morris
In Geoff King and Tanya Krzywinska (eds). *Screenplay: Cinema/Videogames/Interfaces* (London: Wallflower Press, 2002), pp. 81–97.

'Fancy footwork: Walter Benjamin's notes on flânerie'
Rob Shields
In Keith Tester (ed). *The Flâneur* (London: Routledge, 1994), pp. 61–80.

'Introduction'
Robert Lumley
In Robert Lumley (ed). *The Museum Time Machine: Putting Cultures on Display* (London: Routledge, 1988), pp. 1–25.

Film/Television

Torchwood, Russell T. Davies, creator (Cardiff, UK: BBC, 2006)
Doctor Who [New series], Russell T. Davies, creator (Cardiff, UK: BBC, 2005)
Star Trek, Gene Roddenberry, creator (Hollywood, CA: CBS, 1966)

'P.S.', Chris Chibnall, writer *Doctor Who* [New series, web/DVD extra], http://www.bbc.co.uk/programmes/p00zn6ff
'The Angels Take Manhattan', Nick Hurran, dir. *Doctor Who* [New series] (Cardiff, UK: BBC, 2012)
'Rise of the Cybermen', Graeme Harper, dir. *Doctor Who* [New series] (Cardiff, UK: BBC, 2006)

Online
Extracts/Essays/Articles

'*Doctor Who* Experience review'
Louisa Mellor
Den of Geek! 22 February 2011, http://www.denofgeek.com/tv/10292/doctor-who-experience-review

Websites

BBC *Doctor Who* Experience, www.doctorwhoexperience.com/

Chapter 06

The First Time

Paul Booth

For every fan, there must be a time before the fandom started: a time before that fan knew about the show. Every fan's journey into fandom is different, although many may follow similar paths. In my research, I've tried to discover some of the different ways people have become fans, because I'm interested in learning about what makes fans special – and, in the case of this chapter, what makes *Doctor Who* special for fans. It's selfish, really – I've become interested in learning about this because I'm curious about my own pathway into fandom. I've

wanted to find out why I feel the way I do about *Doctor Who*, and why I feel comfortable in a room full of others who feel the same way.

But all fans approach their fandom differently. Some come to the show relatively late in life – perhaps they hadn't heard of the show but a friend convinced them to watch when they were at university. Perhaps some fans grew up without knowing a thing about regeneration or relative dimensions, but caught a glimpse of Matt Smith on BBC America. Or perhaps there are fans who were just a few days old when their parents slipped an 'I <3 <3 the Doctor' onesie on them.

Every fan has a story about 'Their First Time' – the time from which they measure their fandom – Before *Who* and After *Who*: *Who* was your first Doctor? *Who* was your first companion? *When* was your first trip in the TARDIS? And *what* was it about that episode that made it special?

Think about this: how many times have you sat down to watch a television programme and *not* become a fan? How many shows? One hundred? Two hundred? So there must've been something about *Doctor Who* that kept you coming back. Or maybe it wasn't about the show at all, but about the people who watched it with you.

The fans interviewed for this chapter all experienced *Doctor Who*, at some point, for the first time. I interviewed these fans at the 2011 Chicago TARDIS *Doctor Who* fan convention, so while some of these fans share the traditional British teatime experience of watching *Doctor Who*, many of them are American and encountered the show in a different manner. *Doctor Who* first premiered in the United States in 1972, through Time-Life syndication, but it wasn't until public broadcasting stations brought the Tom Baker series over in 1978 that it became more well known. My 'first time', for example, was late one Sunday night on Chicago's Channel 11, my local PBS station.

Although my first experience with the programme was on television, like many of these fans it was significantly augmented by the Target novelizations, which I found every month at the Kane County Flea Market for $1 a book. I devoured each book every month, eagerly going back next month for more. I still have them, of course; I wouldn't dream of getting rid of them (Figure 1).

The fans' answers below illustrate the myriad ways they first experienced the show.

The First Time
Paul Booth

Beyond speaking about their favourite show, however, the fans also note a shift in their own identity, from a time when they *weren't* fans – when they were just viewers settling down to watch something they knew little about – to a time when they were. Of the hundreds of 'first times' for other shows, what is it about *Doctor Who* that struck a chord? In what follows, I let the fans speak for themselves, describing their 'first times' in their own words.[1] Does one of these match your first time? Or is everyone's first time like a fingerprint, similar but different, unique but recognizable?

Fan researchers talk about the 'ritualization' of watching or experiencing the fan's favourite text. For example, Will Brooker has written about *X-Files* fans who all have different rituals when they watch the show. Some like to turn out all the lights and experience the show in complete darkness. Others like to have a particular food item or drink with them when they watch. Sometimes these rituals may be overt and deliberate – turning off the phone so as not to be disturbed – while others may be minute and the fan may not even realize that it is a ritual – sitting in the same spot every week.

But what we don't really talk about (perhaps because it's so hard to remember) is the first time a fan experiences the object that will become their fandom. For fans looking back, it's a moment tinged in nostalgia (see Ivan Phillips's chapter in this volume), but at the time it may be less important than what is being served for tea. The rituals aren't there, the expectations are diminished, the mystery is at its highest. The fan's first time can be an extraordinary event, but only in hindsight.

What's particularly notable about these experiences, I think, is how they are both unique and similar at the same time. No one's 'first time' went exactly the same as another person's, but there is a thread running through them all that connects them. Sometimes it's someone else introducing a friend, family member or roommate to the show. Other times it's a general feeling of 'everyone's talking about this'. Some people may just have been bored and flipping channels, others may have been trying to see for themselves what others were talking about. For many fans it's a childhood memory tinged with nostalgia.

Every fan is different, but each story joins the chorus of others to form a unique fandom. ●

Notes
1. All names as pseudonyms. My thanks to the participants in the study, Jennifer Adams Kelley of Chicago TARDIS, my research assistants Peter Kelly, Calhoun Kersten, and Courtney Neal, my transcriber Nistasha Perez, the DePaul IRB for permission to record the interviews, and the DePaul University Research Council, which helped fund this project.

My dad taped it off of Channel 11 [PBS] back when it was on. We would watch them over and over again. We used to scare the hell out of my sister with some of the episodes. So I'd watch those over and over especially because it was fun to torture her. – Janet

I don't remember not ever having watched Doctor Who. *I was born before* Doctor Who *started. I really don't know when I started watching; I just know that I always knew about it. I remember the last year of William Hartnell, that's when my memories begin a bit. Funnily enough I remember watching* Power of the Daleks *and already knowing about the Daleks but surely I couldn't have watched* The Dalek's Masterplan *then. I have vague memories of it but it might have been of the clip that's on* Blue Peter. *I might have got into* Doctor Who *because of the Dalek manual in the 1960s. – Gareth*

About 1983 or '84. I happened to be babysitting one night and the baby was restless and I just wanted to put something on that was quiet. I was flipping through PBS and it came on. I remember it clearly: It was Ark in Space. *And it's just one of those things that it just kind of... worked. Growing up I had some issues where I felt alien and I felt kind of on the outside, and here was this character who was so amazing and he makes friends everywhere he goes. He never really quite fit in and I think I just identified so strongly with the Doctor that it just was a really good match for me at that time in my life. – Katy*

It was Christmas time, and I was at my cousin's house, and my dad and my uncle were watching The Five Doctors. *And I'm like, 'Hey that looks pretty cool', and I watched it and they all thought I was going to fall asleep and I didn't. I watched it all the way through. – Anne*

The First Time
Paul Booth

A friend of mine in junior high school said you've got to see this strange, British, wobbly-set export that is playing late night on our local PBS station in Minnesota. And the first episode I saw was The Deadly Assassin. *Had no idea what it was. Some time later during a football game, switching channels I saw, for about five seconds,* The Hand of Fear, *and the hand walking inexorably towards someone... and the horrors! It wasn't until much later that I started watching it routinely. — Terry*

It wasn't very good. I was about seven and we had just moved to California. My dad had been watching The Power of Kroll, *with a gigantic octopus and tentacles would come out from anywhere in the water. Even though it was so far away, I remember having a vivid dream seeing this where I was on a playground and it was just raining. I have this memory of this Kroll tentacle coming out and pulling me down the slide. So I was just like, no, no I don't like it. The next episode I saw my dad watching was* Logopolis, *which was just very confusing. So I wasn't into this crazy, curly-haired guy. And then my dad had gotten the* Radio Times *20th Anniversary magazine, and we were in a traffic jam and that was the only thing for me to do. I liked the robot pictures and I wanted to see more. I was just getting to the point in my reading where I could start reading the novelizations, and I think it really helped my reading because I had a visual anchor to the series. So I could deal with the larger words and the paragraphs because I could at least visualize what was going on. And that was why we got our first VCR, because my parents recorded it Saturday nights and then on Sunday dinner we would watch it as a family. And that was our family thing. — Chris*

It has to go back to flipping on the television on a Saturday night back in the mid 80s, finding this unusual looking person walking around with this very long coat and hat and scarf. And then hearing the British accent... And this was unusual for the time: Doctor Who *in Indianapolis was shown on a low power commercial television station that had recently started and needed cheap programming. It was later acquired by the PBS station, which is the typical mechanism back in the 80s for being shown in America. — Richard*

I started watching Doctor Who *in the late 1970s. I was at Northwestern University and a whole bunch of us started watching. Some older people got me into it. Channel 11 [PBS] was showing* Doctor Who. *It was still on Tom Baker, so Tom Baker was my first Doctor. Whoever's your first Doctor is kind of your favourite.* – *Mike*

My first was actually the season opener in 1977. I'm a military brat so we were stationed in England. I think it's 03 September 1977. It was in fact Horror of Fang Rock. *As an introduction when you're 7 years old, you have no idea what's going on but it's really, really cool. And there's this thing coming up the steps and of course I was watching in England which meant 25 minutes a week for a month. I was watching this glowing thing bounce up the stairs in the light house. I have this very vivid memory in the very last episode and I found out years and years later why this happened. Part of Louise Jameson's conditions for returning for that season was that she didn't have to wear the brown contacts anymore. So there's this kind of throwaway line, they watch the explosion, she sees the explosion, and your eyes have changed colors. So for years after that, 'how can watching an explosion make someone's eyes change color', I asked my parents, 'that doesn't make any sense'. - Sarah*

The first episode I was ever shown was because somebody wanted me to write a fanzine story. She showed me Brain of Morbius. *Now people in* Doctor Who *fandom back in the analytical days were like, 'oh no that was an awful episode!' You've got this crazy costuming monster-put-together lurching around. No, no what I saw in that was, Sarah Jane Smith rescues the Doctor. You have a matriarchal society every bit as powerful as the Time Lord society and the Doctor respects these women. And yeah the monsters look weird but it was kind of fun catching those particular spots. And I've just never looked back. – Freema*

My dad was a big fan of the old series. Tried to see if it was as good as he remembered. So he showed us an episode of Tom Baker: The Horror of Fang Rock, *and I was like six. And I just totally didn't get it. It just didn't make sense. That's part of the reason why I didn't rediscover* Doctor Who *until quite a way in the new series, because I had that experience early on. – Bill*

The First Time
Paul Booth

> *I know the one that stays prominent with me is when Peter Davison was regenerating into Colin Baker and I cried. And I guess it was that emotionally attachment to the character. That specific Doctor that made me tear up. – Alex*

> *I remember there was one episode with Tom Baker and you see him going into the Tardis and the Tardis being bigger on the inside and I thought, 'this show is stupid, I'm not going to waste my time with it'. But then I had friends said, 'you need to watch Doctor Who'. And then I wanted to see the regeneration episode. I didn't understand the concept how it worked so I wanted to see it. The Caves of Androzani. During that time, on PBS in Chicago, it was shown on Sunday nights at 11 o'clock and of course I had to go to school the next day so I knew I wasn't going to have an opportunity to watch it, so I taped it. The next day I'm watching the episode and they finally get to the part where the Doctor and Peri get into the Tardis, and a couple of seconds after that the tape cuts out. Missed the whole regeneration sequence! The strange thing about it is, I watched the episode again and again. It was such a great story and I loved watching it. It hooked me to Doctor Who. – David*

> *My parents introduced me to Doctor Who at a very early age, back before I had the opportunity to realize what regeneration was. I was watching a show about the Doctor who was constantly changing character. It took me awhile to realize how there's a whole thing where he changes. And then I went back and started watching it in order. We didn't have public broadcasting, so my aunt was sending all these tapes of Doctor Who. I pretty much grew up with the series. When I started watching it, it was still Colin Baker and Sylvester McCoy. But I remember growing up with Jon Pertwee because it happened we got those tapes first. – Jack*

I recently got in touch with my birth mother after we had our daughter. She talked to me about how I'd enjoy this show Doctor Who. *She gave me an episode to watch and I went home, it was streaming on Netflix and I remember sitting there and watching it and I would say almost, I felt the sort of camaraderie with her. This was this whole universe that I'd just discovered that I'd never even seen or known about and I've been hooked ever since. – Ivy*

I had an older brother and sister. It was something that they would let me do with them, which was an honor for me being so much younger. At that point it was on Friday, Saturday, and Sunday. I could watch on Friday and Saturday but I couldn't watch it on Sunday because I had to go to bed, so every Monday I'd get to ask my brother and sister what happened and they filled me in so I could catch up for next week. – Michael

My best friend and I were in college, and we started watching because we watched Top Gear *on BBC America. I never really wanted to start watching* Doctor Who. *It seemed kind of strange to me. But we decided to sit down and start watching the 5th season [2010]. We figured we'd just stuck it up and watch it and then after that okay now let's watch the second, let's watch the third and suddenly it was a marathon where we became obsessed and we had to go back and watch all the others together. – Michelle*

You know I wasn't a fan of Doctor Who *at all before 2005. I'd seen the TV Movie. I had seen it on PBS as a kid. It was something my grandparents thrust me in front of to babysit me and I was an extreme literalist as a child. I was very critical of the show. They keep changing the actor and thinking us kids are too stupid to notice. The Daleks are on wheels and K9 is on wheels therefore K9 is working with the Daleks and the Doctor should realize that. It was really extreme realism and literalism. – Sophie*

The First Time
Paul Booth

> The first episode I watched was 'The Doctor's Wife'. I'd been a big fan of [Neil] Gaiman, and I just thought the show was amazing. I just instantly connected. I thought it was hilarious and heart-wrenching. I went back and watched all the other episodes and I clicked with the characters so much and I've never felt this emotionally attached to a show. It's kind of silly but at the same time I don't really care 'cause I love it that much. – Grace

> It felt so organic being sucked into Doctor Who. I had heard a lot of people talking about Doctor Who for a long time; I just never knew what it was. When people explained to me, it went way over my head. So I finally said, 'you know what, screw this, I'm going to actually go and get some DVDs'. One of my friends joined in. She was a big fan, she was like, 'I need to be there with you when you're watching this'. First episode was kind of weird, but it's cool 'cause the episode resembled Power Rangers. I'm not even kidding. The monsters looked a lot like Power Rangers. And then towards the second episode, this is definitely cool. And then after the third, forth, fifth – by halfway through the first season I said, 'I love this show'. Pretty soon we ended up watching thirteen straight hours of it. We didn't stop. We just finished the entire season and I'm like okay where are the next ones. I suddenly realized oh my gosh this thing has suddenly taken hold. I really love this thing. – Amy

> It's very hard to extricate a single experience out of my DNA. I feel like I sort of live and breathe Doctor Who. I was one of those people who said I'm so excited for it to come back because the torch needs to be passed. It can't be just guys who are aging out and just hanging out. But we're going to hand it on. It's not going to be for us. In that first season Christopher Eccleston's Doctor had an amazing arc where he was damaged and he sort of began to be healing through his emotions with Rose and this was the unbelievable start to the new series. For me that just blew me away. I could not conceive of the Doctor like this. It was just the greatest thing ever. – Patrick

~~~~~~~~~~

GO FURTHER

Books

Time on TV: Temporal Displacement and Mashup Television
Paul Booth
(New York: Peter Lang, 2012)

Digital Fandom: New Media Studies
Paul Booth
(New York: Peter Lang, 2010)

Extracts/Essays/Articles

'A sort of homecoming: Fan viewing and symbolic pilgrimage'
Will Brooker
In Jonathan Gray, Cornel Sandvoss and C. Lee Harrington (eds). *Fandom: Identities and Communities in a Mediated World* (New York: New York University Press, 2007), pp. 149–64.

Film/Television

Top Gear [New series], Andy Wilman, executive producer (London, UK: BBC, 2002)
Doctor Who [Classic series], Sydney Newman and Verity Lambert, creators (London, UK: BBC, 1963); [New series], Russell T. Davies, creator (Cardiff, UK: BBC, 2005)
Blue Peter, John Hunter Blair, creator (London, UK: BBC, 1958)

'The Doctor's Wife', Richard Clark, dir. *Doctor Who* [New series] (Cardiff, UK: BBC, 2011)
Doctor Who: The Movie, Geoffrey Sax, dir. *Doctor Who* [Classic series] (Hollywood, CA: Fox and London, UK: BBC, 1996)
The Caves of Androzani, Graeme Harper, dir. *Doctor Who* [Classic series] (London, UK: BBC, 1984)
The Five Doctors, Peter Moffatt, dir. *Doctor Who* [Classic series] (London, UK: BBC, 1983)
The Power of Kroll, Norman Stewart, dir. *Doctor Who* [Classic series] (London, UK: BBC, 1978–79)
The Horror of Fang Rock, Paddy Russell, dir. *Doctor Who* [Classic series] (London, UK: BBC, 1977)

The First Time
Paul Booth

The Deadly Assassin, David Maloney, dir. *Doctor Who* [Classic series] (London, UK: BBC, 1976)

The Brain of Morbius, Christopher Barry, dir. *Doctor Who* [Classic series] (London, UK: BBC, 1976)

The Ark in Space, Rodney Bennett, dir. *Doctor Who* [Classic series] (London, UK: BBC, 1975)

The Power of the Daleks, Christopher Barry, dir. *Doctor Who* [Classic series] (London, UK: BBC, 1966)

The Daleks' Masterplan, Douglas Camfield, dir. *Doctor Who* [Classic series] (London, UK: BBC, 1965–66)

Part 2
What Do
Doctor Who Fans
Do?

Chapter
07

Do It Yourself:
Women, Fanzines and
Doctor Who

Leslie McMurtry

→ According to Paul Cornell in 1997, the general public would find 'the idea of magazines produced on an amateur basis extremely improbable'. Nonetheless, not only do *Doctor Who* fanzines exist, they exist in great numbers. Wading into fanzine history is a thorny thicket, and geographical as well as chronological distance makes a broad overview of the subject virtually impossible. What might have been true for *Doctor Who* fanzines in the United States in the mid-1980s - where many women edited, illustrated and wrote - was quite atypical for the fanzine writers and editors in Britain in the 1990s - where often female fans were treated as a rare and alien species. And different again for the scene of specialized fanzines in Australia and New Zealand where women's voices were plentiful. And different again in the post-Internet fandom of today.

Fig. 1: The editing staff behind *Jelly Baby Chronicles*. (©Paulie Gilmore (1983); *Doctor Who* ©BBC).

As Frederick Wertham recorded in 1973, Mary Celeste Kearney in 2006 and Brigid Cherry in 2010, fanzine production and *Doctor Who* fandom have both been dominated by 'male, middle-class, white' fans. Nevertheless, female *Doctor Who* fanzine participants have always existed. The content of pre-2005 fanzines suggests two fan attitudes: the feminine fan and the nominally-female, or as I term it, 'gender-blind', fan. The feminine fan was one who, simply put, was aware of her femininity and allowed this quality to permeate her work: she might not always trumpet the fact she was female, but she never sought to hide it. Alternatively, Jackie Jenkins typifies the 'gender-blind' fan, whose writing does not speak to the female – much less to the feminine – experience and utilizes a homogenized 'Who-speak'. Despite received wisdom, the tide has not turned completely towards 'feminine' *Who* writing post-2005, though those who write in that mode often do so self-deprecatingly.

A whiff of old boys' club

Doctor Who has stereotypically been an all-male preserve, yet some writers have claimed, as Hickman has, that *Doctor Who* has always had an inherent appeal to women (Figure 1). *Kate* Orman suggested in Doctor Who Magazine (*DWM*) in 2005 that the lack of romance in the Classic series 'freed girls to try other things'. One strategy for appropriating *Doctor Who* was through allusion or play, adopting a position of increased femininity to identify with the overtly feminine companions. According to Orman, Sara Kingdom, a take-charge, militaristic woman, would have appealed to playground-age girls. Jo Grant, Liz Shaw, Sarah Jane Smith, Romana and Nyssa, as 'working women', might appeal to girls in late childhood. Rie (Meyer) Sheridan Rose obviously capitalized on Sarah Jane's appeal and the sense of fan identification when she edited the popular US fanzine *From the Notebook of Sarah Jane*.

Further, Jackie Marshall suggests, radically for the time, that Tegan's devotion to the Fifth Doctor is romantic love. Since the 'majority of females questioned would quite

Do It Yourself: Women, Fanzines and *Doctor Who*
Leslie McMurtry

definitely have fancied him [the Fifth Doctor]', Marshall's association is one particularly feminine way of engaging with the text. Elizabeth Burak, writing originally in *Eye of Orion* in 1999, identified with New Adventures companion Bernice Summerfield as representing the 'anti-Barbie-doll approach to female teachers'. Orman also conjectures that girls might be tempted to identify with the 'bad girls' of *Who*, such as the Rani and Captain Wrack from *Enlightenment* (Cumming, 1983, Season 20). All this seems to underline that there are more ways for a girl *Who* fan to identify than the simple feminized-companion/Doctor dichotomy.

Do it yourself

It is a pervasive fallacy that fanzines (that is, fan magazines) arrived on the scene in the late 1970s with the punk movement. Frederic Wertham has traced them back as far as 1930. As fanzines 'in their most basic form, require only paper, writing implements, and elementary compositional skills', girls have self-published fan magazines since the 1930s, as Mary Celeste Kearney pointed out in her book *Girls Make Media* (2006).

Meanwhile, according to Brian J. Robb, organized *Doctor Who* fandom began in 1965 with the William Hartnell Fan Club. The *Doctor Who* Appreciation Society (DWAS) was founded in 1976, and by 1980, fan clubs and fan literature were being produced outside of Britain. *Gallifrey, Ark in Space, Frontier Worlds, Aggedor, Cygnus Alpha, Shada, Wheel in Space* and *Space Rat* are just some of the many titles from the late 1970s and mid-1980s, along with the official DWAS newsletter, *Celestial Toyroom*. These earliest fanzines existed to contemplate the series itself, while later fanzines offered, in Robb's words, 'an outlet for experimentation'.

Women's presence is not obvious in early *Celestial Toyroom* copies, but interestingly, they dominate the pen pal columns. According to Ron North in *Celestial Toyroom* in 1983, *Images* was the first (British) *Doctor Who* fanzine edited by a woman, with *Space Rat* being the second (edited by Jackie Marshall and Val Douglas, later to edit *Queen Bat*). He was mistaken, however; Linda Williams and Geraldine Landen pre-empted these titles. Debates in *Aggedor* in 1984, *Celestial Toyroom/TARDIS* in 1986 and *Queen Bat* in 1987 centred on women's roles in *Doctor Who* rather than in fandom. John Nathan-Turner was *Doctor Who*'s producer in 1980 and was originally on good terms with the editors of Doctor Who *Bulletin* (DWB); their falling out created a fanzine whirlpool. *The Frame, Purple Haze* and *Cottage Under Siege* (the first openly gay *Who* fanzine) arose out of the resulting cultures and counter-cultures.

The situation was somewhat different in North America, due to many factors but crystallizing around a fandom that was, in Kathleen Toth's words, 'distinctly older', meaning an average age of 30. Jody Lynn Nye stressed in *Chicks Dig Time Lords* (2010) that most fans she met were female, and writer Kathryn Sullivan was representative of this kind of fandom, encountering her first fanzine at MediaWest*Con 1 in Lansing, Michigan in 1981. Wayne Rooper in a 2000 issue of *Shockeye's Kitchen* went on at length about

Fig. 2: 'The woman who came
to the tavern'. (©Private Lives
(1992); Doctor Who ©BBC).

this difference, saying some British fans were guilty of being 'po-faced and painfully sanctimonious', and both he and Michael Burgess, writing in *Metamorph* 1993, seemed to agree that, in effect, female fans bring in badly-needed humour and were sorely missed in British fandom.

American fanzines were often twice as long as British ones, and virtually every North American fanzine title from the 1980s was edited by a woman, with art and fiction provided by both sexes. Paulie Gilmore, editor of *Jelly Baby Chronicles* from 1983, did much of her own artwork and fiction-writing as well as contributing to other 'zines; issue three from 1984 featured a portfolio from Cheryl Whitfield Duval, who edited two fanzines of her own, *Time Log* and *Rassilon's Star*, and published a vast quantity of art and writing in other titles. Meanwhile, in Australia, a similar gender parity was at work, with Sarah Prefect joking in a 1985 issue of *Cloister Bell* that she would trigger a mass wave of immigration when she announced that the male:female ratio of fans aged fifteen to twenty-five was almost 1:1. It is unclear whether this was the case in New Zealand, with Rochelle Thickpenny – later assistant editor of the New Zealand *Doctor Who* Fan Club fanzine *Time/Space Visualiser* – writing in 1992, 'you ever notice how girls are in the minority when it comes to liking *Doctor Who*?'

A rare breed?

A shift seemed to occur in the late 1980s and early 1990s in British fandom, coinciding with the demise of *Queen Bat*. In 1991, for example, fan Karen Dunn was called 'an unusual phenomenon' at the Fitzroy Tavern, according to the Tav-based 'zine *Private Lives*. *Private Lives*, which arrived in the wake of cross-fandom cooperation along with *Brave New World*, *Alien Corn*, *Top*, *Club Tropicana* and *Circus*, features a back cover cartoon in 1992 of 'The woman who came to the tavern', emphasizing her isolation and horror (Figure 2). Dunn wrote about her experience in 2009 in *The Terrible Zodin*, 'There was nothing more likely to bring the Juke Box at the Fitzroy Tavern scraping to a halt than a woman in a Tom Baker T-shirt strolling in and offering the barman a jelly baby.' Moreover, as North American fandom participation slowed down, female contributors to British 'zines grew scarce.

Fanfiction was written by both men and women. Indeed, male writers dominated DWAS's fiction 'zine *Cosmic Masque* until the 1990s. Women writers did show a particular affinity for 'mashups', from Clare Ford's *Doctor Who* and *Blake's 7* (Nation, BBC, 1978–81) work in *Queen Bat* (1985) to Cheryl Whitfield Duval's book-length, self-illustrated combination of *Doctor Who* and *Amadeus*, *Sing Sweetly, Sing Strong* (1990). Catherine Siemann contributed the truly prescient comic 'The epic of *Doctor Who*', in which Hollywood execs ruin *Doctor Who*, in *Jelly Baby Chronicles* (1983).

Bafflegab is one United States fanzine which brought an unashamedly feminine

Do It Yourself: Women, Fanzines and *Doctor Who*
Leslie McMurtry

touch to *Who* fan writing. 'Uncensored scenes we'd love to see' by Cheryl Whitfield Duval is an energized flight of fancy showing romantic scenes between a variety of Doctor/companion pairs (Figure 3). In 1986, Audrey Baker lambasted the majority of fanfiction writers in *Queen Bat*, scorning 'The Romantic' (Mary Sue), 'The Adult' (sexual 'shipping'), and slash for 'offloading [the writer's] own daydreams' on us. Val Douglas defended fanfiction after Baker's assault, suggesting it was written 'because we girls aren't exactly well-catered for where dirty books are concerned'. If fanzines such as *Bafflegab* were, in riot grrrl chronicler Teal Triggs's words, 'a safe space to poke fun at men', the 1999 erotic fanfiction anthology edited by Lori Grenci, *Warm Gallifreyan Nights*, took the feminine aspect one step further – and earned the sharp scorn of male fans, as Orman reports.

Gender-neutral content like poetry and filks (science fiction song parodies) were supplemented by nonfiction from a female perspective. Deborah Morton's 'Pulp friction' in *Shockeye's Kitchen* 12 is a column about her *Who*-obsessed boyfriend and his wall of merchandise with references to naughty themed games, and signed '♥ Debs xx'. In *Who* fanzines, even those with content by women, symbols like ♥ are extremely rare, though Jackie Marshall advertised for her upcoming fanzine *Space Rat* in 1982 by placing an ad in *Celestial Toyroom* imitating the style of a cross-stitch pattern. Certainly rare are what might be termed feminist tracts; one such is Sarah Groenewegen's 1997 'Frocks, coats, and dress (non)sense' from *Bog Off!*, what Cornell termed the 'determinedly radical' Australian 'zine. This piece not only identifies (with reluctance, given Groenewegen's resistance to labels) the author as a lesbian *Who* fan, it also highlights the problems of cross-dressing within sci-fi fandoms.

Jackie Jenkins and the 'gender-blind' fandom
In 1990, Vanessa Bishop wrote the poem 'Oh! To be a fanboy' in the pages of *Purple Haze*. There is nothing gender-, or orientation-specific, about the poem; it's about the fan convention experience, as encapsulated in the all-embracing line, 'Cor, I fancy her, I fancy him.' However, fanzine editor Alistair McGown's response, reprinted immediately afterwards by Cornell in *Licence Denied!* (1997), was inspired by the *photos* of Bishop as much as anything she wrote. Further, both Jenkins and Orman indicate they have been many times assumed to be lesbians by mere dint of being female *Who* fans. Jenkins, though heterosexual, mostly prefers to keep gender out of *Doctor Who*, and Orman, self-confessed '*gender non-conforming*', dislikes the persistent assumptions (original emphasis).

Gender non-conforming is at the heart of Jackie Jenkins, the pseudonymous female *Who* writer commissioned by Gary Gillatt in 1997 to be *DWM*'s 'trendy' answer to Bridget Jones. Although Jenkins never wrote in a fanzine, I use her experience and style of writing to stand for the gender-blind fan writer. She may have been, in Gillatt's words, 'the

Fig. 4: 'Read the book, Adric'.
(©Hannah Rothman and
Kaleigh Chambers (2011);
Doctor Who ©BBC).

greatest writer about *Doctor Who* there has ever been', but she was also 'still' a girl. This is exactly how she was introduced in *DWM* 251 in May 1997. 'Why can't people,' Jenkins asks in *Chicks Dig Time Lords* (2010), 'remember me for me?'

Jenkins is a female fan who resists being dragged into the spotlight as female and would rather pursue her fannishness in a prose made up of experiences that are gender-neutral. She epitomizes what Brigid Cherry calls '*Who* speak', derived from the early years of *Doctor Who* fanzines, Terrance Dicks's Target novel descriptions, production terms, self-deprecating language and acronyms. '*Who* speak' is used in gender-neutral fanzine content, which I would argue is the dominant mode of pre-2005 female *Who* fanzine writers. '*Who* speak' also came in handy in parody (Figure 4). In *Queen Bat*, Audrey Baker's 'The Doctor as a sexpot' was against the Doctor being sexual on-screen, and 'Who's a naughty boy' by Val Douglas was a firmly tongue-in-cheek response, as was her poem about Susan, 'Oh no! We mustn't mention her'.

The dominant expression of gender-blind fandom was in analytical/ critical/fandom pieces, ranging from Jackie Roe's report on the Manchester Fan Olympiad in 1991 in *Private Lives* to Amanda Murray's piece on 'Pertwee' from *DWB*. Vanessa Bishop embodies this writing at its best, and her fan journey is described in *Licence Denied!* in terms virtually identical to a male fan's. When she says, 'I love everything about Tom Baker down to the cilia of his nostrils,' we know this is not a particularly feminized love.

Fandom regenerates

Post-1991, due to the open submissions policies of the New Adventures and the inclusive principles of *DWM* editors John Freeman, Gary Russell and Gary Gillatt, writing for fanzines was seen as less prestigious, because the poachers were turning gamekeepers, so to speak. The Noughties were also seen as, in Robin Barnard's words from the first issue of *Panic Moon*, 'seemingly the dying days of the printed fanzine, with the Internet cemented as the hub of fandom.' As Robb reported, by 2008, fanzines were 'few and far between', with *Whotopia, Enlightenment* (fanzine of Canada's *Doctor Who* Information Network), *Myth Makers* (a fiction 'zine also produced by DWIN), *Celestial Toyroom, Time/Space Visualiser* and *Live from Mars* soldiering on.

Nevertheless, a 'fanzine renaissance' became manifest from about that year; the 'resurgence in fanzines' is described by Daniel Gee, editor of *Fish Fingers and Custard* (*FFAC*) in 2010. Along with *FFAC*, the other 'zines to be described in this influx were *Shooty Dog Thing, Rassilon's Rod* and *Blue Box*. Certainly the hard-copy 'zines were celebrated for their authenticity against their 'posh PDF cousins', as *Blue Box*'s David MacGowan put it. *Rassilon's Rod*, in particular, was celebrated for being, in Paul Castle's

Do It Yourself: Women, Fanzines and *Doctor Who*
Leslie McMurtry

words, 'deliberately retro', unconsciously echoing the 'cut-n-paste aesthetic' of riot gr-rrl publications like *Kitten Scratches*.

Much more visibly than the changes going on within fanzines, the incursion of female fans en masse, post-2005, as described by Lizbeth Myles, is linked to the 'rise of the fangirl'. Robb identifies this increase in female fans with David Tennant. The perceived sexiness of Tennant was no doubt, as Wallace notes, used as a marketing tool for the 2006 series, but if, as Jackie Jenkins suggests in 2008, 'Tennant happened and suddenly every woman in the office is a dyed-in-the-wool fan', post-2005 fanzines are surprisingly mute on this point. Perhaps the silence is due to what Wertham affectionately described as the 'sincere and spontaneous' writing that once characterized fanzines migrating to pseudonymous blogs and messageboards, with fiction retreating to LiveJournal and *A Teaspoon and an Open Mind*. The most in-depth fanzine study on the feelings and values of 'Tennant fangirls' was conducted by the male editor of *FFAC* in 2010. This piece was a series of interviews with six self-described 'fangirls', who challenged the stereotypes. They could not agree on a favourite Tenth Doctor story nor on a reason why they admired and lusted after Tennant so much. All participants except two agreed Tennant's good looks were 'icing on the cake' to his other qualities. Julie Chaston in *Enlightenment* in 2010 wrote an elegy to Tennant that said absolutely nothing about his looks or sex appeal.

The second reason given is, in Robb's words, the show's new 'emotional intelligence'. Men and women have remarked on the changes wrought in fan discourse. 'Genuine love and passion and human interest in the Tardis [sic]? YES PLEASE!' David MacGowan wrote in *Blue Box*. This emotional intelligence has caused some female fans to abandon 'gender-blind' and invest more of their femininity in their writing. Katie Steely-Brown in *FFAC* 11 is able to discuss romance in New *Who* as part of a larger, more gender-neutral appeal of *Doctor Who* to a (presumably) North American audience. Abby Peck seems to reclaim Sarah Jane as almost a heroine for the riot grrrl movement. Emma Donovan and Chloe Hardy let loose torrents of 'fangirlish' emotion on the pages of *FFAC*, a refreshing and representative contrast that marks it as uniquely post-2005. There is a certain amount of playful self-deprecation in writing like this which seems to echo one of the elements of '*Who* speak' detailed above.

Certainly, too, analytical and critical writing are well represented by female writers such as Fiona Moore, Amanda Barton, Karen Davies and Deborah Stanish; Lloyd Rose and Nina Kolunovsky in *Enlightenment*; Lisa Parker and Lydia Butz in *Panic Moon*; Aya Vandenbussche, Lori Jansen, Evan Keraminas, Deborah Taylor, Hannah Rothman and Leslie McMurtry in *The Terrible Zodin*; and Elizabeth Peloso, Lisa Carroll and Caron Lindsay in *FFAC*. Editor Lea distributes fanzine *Venusian Spearmint* in the Fitzroy Tavern 'in the attempt,' she says, 'to keep the old traditions alive in the Internet age of blogs and Twitter'. Artwork by female fans has positively exploded in post-2005 fanzines, including *Panic Moon* (whose writers are 90 per cent male), *The Terrible Zodin* and *FFAC* (which has included a piece by Tabitha Mounteer on 'How to make a TARDIS blanket'). Even if male fans such as Paul Castle have admitted to wanting to craft a K9 soft toy out of denim, it seems unlikely a pre-2005 fanzine would have included a craft feature in its pages, except to ridicule it. Meanwhile, the comics fanzine *Vworp Vworp*, released in 2009 and edited by Gareth Kavanagh and Colin Brockhurst, has as yet had no female contributors. Orman found in 2010 that *DWM*'s survey respondents are still 71 per cent male.

Conclusion

'A fanzine is something that people do together,' wrote Daniel Gee in 2010. Even in 2012, fanzines maintain their essence of 'newness' which the editor of *Hippycore* linked with underground punk fanzines in Paul Rutherford's *Fanzine Culture* (1992). Graeme Burk and Robert Smith?, editors of *Time, Unincorporated* (2010–11), have suggested that the Internet has actually caused the fanzine to flourish once more. Whether at the forefront or the fringes, whether hidden by a mirage of 'those limp, greasy-haired young men' as Brigid Cherry called them in 1989, or providing covers, editing and writing for a fanzine, female *Doctor Who* fanzine participants are present. Stanish has repeatedly likened the way boys approach sci-fi to baseball statistics. As for the girls, she says in *Enlightenment* 135, 'they may be looking for something different in the show […] but they are just as committed'. In *Aggedor* 5 (1984), Pam Baddeley suggested that the reason men dominated *Who* fandom was because 'women are educated to relate to people more than to abstract concepts'. Perhaps there is also a confusion of terms; Kim Dickson wrote in 1996 that 'current estimates say that at least 10 per cent of the population, when pressed, will admit to enjoying *Doctor Who*, but don't identify as *Doctor Who* fans'. Is and should *Doctor Who* fanzine writing be 'sexless'? It's a question that will continue to be discussed as long as there are fanzines, and though their deaths have been predicted many times, they do what the Doctor does best: keep on regenerating.

Grateful acknowledgments to Jamie Beckwith, Robbie Bourget, Cheryl Duval, Matthew Kilburn, Rie Sheridan Rose, Kathryn Sullivan and Deb Walsh. Some *Doctor Who* fanzines are occasionally available on eBay (such as *Console Room*, *Bafflegab*, *Jelly Baby Chronicles* and *Private Lives*). I was fortunate enough to be able to consult several fan-run 'archives' that included some of the older print fanzines (such as *Celestial Toyroom*, *Frontier Worlds*, *Queen Bat* and *Space Rat*). Below are links to databases and indices of some of the older paper fanzines. ●

Do It Yourself: Women, Fanzines and *Doctor Who*
Leslie McMurtry

~~~~~~~~~~~~~~

GO FURTHER

Books

Single White Who *Fan: The Life and Times of Jackie Jenkins*
Jackie Jenkins
(Andover: Hirst Books, 2011)

Time, Unincorporated: The Doctor Who *Fanzine Archives: Vol. 2: Writings on the Classic*
Series and *Vol. 3: Writings on the New Series*
Graeme Burk and Robert Smith? (eds)
(Des Moines: Mad Norwegian Press, 2010-11)

(The Best of) Shooty Dog Thing
Paul Castle
(Andover: Hirst Books, 2010)

Timeless Adventures: How Doctor Who *Conquered TV*
Brian J. Robb
(Harpenden: Kamera Books, 2009)

'Do It Yourself' Girl Revolution: Ladyfest, Performance, and Fanzine Culture
Teal Triggs
(London: London College of Communication, 2009)

Girls Make Media
Mary Celeste Kearney
(London: Routledge, 2006)

Licence Denied!: Rumblings from the Doctor Who *Underground*
Paul Cornell (ed)
(London: Virgin Books, 1997)

Fanzine Culture
Paul Rutherford
(Glasgow: Clydesdale Press, 1992)

The World of Fanzines: A Special Form of Communication
Frederic Wertham
(Carbondale: Southern Illinois Press, 1973)

Extracts/Essays/Articles

'The importance of being brilliant'
Julie Chaston
In Graeme Burk and Robert Smith? (eds). *Time, Unincorporated: The* Doctor Who *Fanzine Archives: Vol. 3: Writings on the New Series* (Des Moines: Mad Norwegian Press, 2011), pp. 167–70.

'Foreword'
Gary Gillatt
In *Single White* Who *Fan: The Life and Times of Jackie Jenkins* (Andover: Hirst Books, 2011), pp. 7–10.

'The shipping news' and 'It's not you, it's me'
Deborah Stanish
In Graeme Burk and Robert Smith? (eds). *Time, Unincorporated: The* Doctor Who *Fanzine Archives: Vol. 3: Writings on the New Series* (Des Moines: Mad Norwegian Press, 2011), pp. 111–14; pp. 286–88.

'Benny accolade'
Elizabeth Burak
In Paul Castle (ed). *(The Best of) Shooty Dog Thing* (Andover: Hirst Books, 2010), pp. 53–57.

'Squee, retcon, fanwank and the not-we: Computer-mediated discourse and the online audience for nuwho'
Brigid Cherry
In Christopher J. Hansen (ed). *Ruminations, Peregrinations, and Regenerations: A Critical Approach to* Doctor Who (Newcastle: Cambridge Scholars Publishing, 2010), pp. 209–34.

'Being Jackie Jenkins: Memoirs from a parallel universe'
Jackie Jenkins
In Lynne M. Thomas and Tara O'Shea (eds). *Chicks Dig Time Lords: A Celebration of* Doctor Who *by the Women Who Love It* (Des Moines: Mad Norwegian Press, 2010), pp. 23–30.

'Hopelessly devoted to *Who*'
Jody Lynn Nye
In Lynne M. Thomas and Tara O'Shea (eds). *Chicks Dig Time Lords: A Celebration of* Doctor Who *by the Women Who Love It* (Des Moines: Mad Norwegian Press, 2010), pp. 103–11.

Do It Yourself: Women, Fanzines and *Doctor Who*
Leslie McMurtry

'My fandom regenerates'
Deborah Stanish
In Lynne M. Thomas and Tara O'Shea (eds). *Chicks Dig Time Lords: A Celebration of* Doctor Who *by the Women Who Love It* (Des Moines: Mad Norwegian Press, 2010), pp. 31–37.

'The fanzine factor'
Kathryn Sullivan
In Lynne M. Thomas and Tara O'Shea (eds). *Chicks Dig Time Lords: A Celebration of* Doctor Who *by the Women Who Love It* (Des Moines: Mad Norwegian Press, 2010), pp. 122–32.

'Editor's page'
Clayton Hickman
Doctor Who *Magazine* 362. 5 November 2005, p. 3.

'Girls allowed'
Kate Orman
Doctor Who *Magazine;* 362. 5 November 2005, pp. 15–21.

'Oh! to be a fanboy' and 'My Noddy holder badge'
Vanessa Bishop
In Paul Cornell (ed). *Licence Denied!: Rumblings from the* Doctor Who *Underground* (London: Virgin Books, 1997), pp. 61–64; pp. 76–78.

'Frocks, coats, and dress (non)sense'
Sarah J Groenewegen
In Paul Cornell (ed). *Licence Denied!: Rumblings from the* Doctor Who *Underground* (London: Virgin Books, 1997), pp. 73–76.

'Together-ness'
Alistair McGown
In Paul Cornell (ed). *Licence Denied!: Rumblings from the* Doctor Who *Underground* (London, UK: Virgin Books, 1997), pp. 64–65.

'Pertwee'
Amanda Murray
In Paul Cornell (ed). *Licence Denied!: Rumblings from the* Doctor Who *Underground* (London, UK: Virgin Books, 1997), pp. 21–28.

Film/Television

Blake's 7, Terry Nation, creator (London, BBC: 1979)
Doctor Who [Classic series], Sydney Newman and Verity Lambert, creators (London, UK: BBC, 1963)

Enlightenment, Fiona Cumming, dir. *Doctor Who* [Classic series] (London, UK: BBC, 1983)

Online
Websites

Archive: Time/Space Visualiser, http://nzdwfc.tetrap.com/archive/
'Is that a TARDIS in your closet?' by Kim Dickson (1996), *Happiness Patrol*, http://www.reocities.com/Area51/Lair/8022/HappinessPatrol1.html#Kim
'Journeys by fanzine' by Nick Cooper (1997), http://www.625.org.uk/staraker/st04jbyf.htm
'Burnt Toast', *Tabula Rasa*, http://www.tabula-rasa.info/BurntToast/
Classic Genzine Fanfiction Archive, http://www.debwalsh.com/fanficarchive/authors.html
'*Doctor Who* fanzines', *Fan History*, http://www.fanhistory.com/wiki/Doctor_Who_fanzines
The Doctor Who *fanzine database*, http://web.archive.org/web/20070927212729/the-fanzinedatabase.tvheaven.com/a-z.htm
The Doctor Who *fanzine preservation project*, http://homepages.bw.edu/~jcurtis/dwfpp.htm
'List of *Doctor Who* fanzines', *Fanlore*, http://fanlore.org/wiki/List_of_Doctor_Who_Fanzines

'We're Making Our Own Happy Ending!': The *Doctor Who* Fan Vidding Community

Katharina Freund

→ If someone were to watch *Doctor Who* fan videos (or vids) without having seen the series itself, she might get the impression that the series is a dark, angst-ridden romance or drama. Fan vidding can best be understood as a type of visual fanfiction. Video editors, known as vidders, adapt and alter footage from their favourite television shows with a piece of music in order to focus on elements they find more desirable, such as particular relationships or characters. While *Doctor Who* can be said to straddle many different genres, it was originally created with a family audience in mind and still maintains a cross-generational appeal, as noted by Matt Hills in *Triumph of a Time Lord* (2010).

With the New series beginning in 2005, executive producer Russell T. Davies brought a distinctly more melodramatic air, although the family-oriented and 'monster-of-the-week' elements were still prominent. For the community of fan vidders, though, it is the character-driven drama/romantic story that interests them the most. This chapter will introduce the practice of vidding, and describe how vids alter the original footage in order to make the text better suit the fannish interests of the vidding community. I will briefly describe the history of vidding in the pre-digital age before moving to discuss how vidders understand their practice as a gendered intervention in the televisual text. I will then analyse three particular *Doctor Who* vids as exemplars of how vidders engage with the series in different ways.

The practice of vidding

While there are many different remix communities, *Doctor Who* fan vidders primarily interact using the online blogging and social networking site LiveJournal. As I describe in *Veni, Vidi, Vids* (2012), vidding is heavily female-dominated, with over 90 per cent of vidders on LiveJournal identifying as female. Vidders also tend to be white, English speaking, and from the United States, United Kingdom or another Western European country. These vidders are an extremely media-savvy audience: they are avid watchers of television and consumers of popular culture. Using digital editing technology, vidders are able to re-edit the footage of television series and film and re-organize it into a narrative which is more in line with their fannish interests. Fans engage in vidding for themselves, and they are generally not intended for an audience beyond other vidders and fans. Contemporary vidders share their vids through a variety of platforms including the streaming sites YouTube, Vimeo and Blip.tv, as well as Twitter and Tumblr.

Struggle over meaning

As Henry Jenkins wrote in his canonical study *Textual Poachers* (1992):

Because popular narratives often fail to satisfy, fans must struggle with them, to try to articulate to themselves and others unrealized possibilities within the original works. Because the texts continue to fascinate, fans cannot dismiss them from their attention but rather must try to find ways to salvage them for their interests.

While Jenkins's work has been critiqued by scholars such as Matt Hills, in my discussions with fans they often used a similar language of resistance and re-writing to describe how they understood their vidding practices.

For example, at a vidding convention I attended in the United Kingdom several vidders explained their motivation thusly:

'We're Making Our Own Happy Ending!':
The *Doctor Who* Fan Vidding Community
Katharina Freund

V1: I think we have the same impulse as [fan] fic writers, we wanna fix things, we wanna see what we wanna see.
V2: The best stories do come out of frustration.
V3: Yeah, it's more like that loving a character and just trying to develop something that is on the show [*sic*], sometimes they don't have the time to address this particular character very deeply or it's just scattered everywhere and you just wanna put it together.

During a discussion regarding *Doctor Who* vids, a Welsh vidder explained that her desire to vid was in part a response to how certain storylines (particularly involving Donna in Series 4) had developed: 'It's like the producers don't seem to realize, to really realize, what they've done and it felt to me like the fans were trying to say, "No, look, *this* is what you've done to the characters"'. As noted by the American vidding fan quoted below, vids emphasize particular emotional components of a series:

Vids are boiled down. Vids are poetry where the show is the 19th century novel in 5 volumes. Vids often boil something down to their essence. Take away everything except the expressions and just look at this crucial little shimmering drop and that's wonderful.

Vidders also commonly point out that the desire to vid is linked to their position as female audience members and fans: as a mostly female audience, the desire to vid was linked with a perceived lack of storylines and characters which appeal to women.

We [women] don't get to see the stories we want to see. Most TV and certainly movies are done for a male audience, eighteen to thirty-four [...] and they are not making the entertainments we necessarily want to see. We see all these other texts inside these things. So we have to take what's given to us and instead show the world how we see it; I'm going to make what I want to see. I think, from my personal experience, that female fans tend to form these sorts of close relationships with the characters and that often leads to wanting to do vidding.

The key way that vids act to change the original source material is by playing with generic conventions to evoke the mood desired by the vidder. While the actual definition of genre is contested, it generally is taken to mean 'type' or 'kind', and refers to a specific set of conventions, features and norms that delineate a specific group of texts, as noted by Jason Mittell in his 2004 book, *Genre and Television*. Viewers are trained from a young age to recognize genre categories, which are culturally constructed. *Doctor Who* intersects with many different television genres: the Classic series was generally understood as a sci-fi adventure series with a family audience in mind, and New

Fig. 1: A screenshot from
'My skin' showing the Ninth
Doctor. (©raspberry_splat;
Doctor Who ©BBC).

Fig. 2: The Tenth Doctor in
'My skin'. (©raspberry_splat;
Doctor Who ©BBC).

Who also has significant romantic, dramatic, and comedic elements and subplots strewn throughout.

While some have a background in film studies or television production, in general vidders rely on their media literacies of genre conventions as television fans to craft their vids. As indicated in the quotations above, vids tend to focus on one particular element of the text and explore it in more depth than the original was able to.

The most popular types of vids, however, are those that focus on characters (known as 'character studies') and on relationships between characters (relationship or "shipper' vids). These vids explore character motivations, back stories, loves, friendships, relationships and other interpersonal and character-driven elements, regardless of the focus of the original source material. Minor or supporting characters are often given centre stage in vids, and are developed more thoroughly than in the original source.

Another of the common vid types is the character study, which focuses on the emotions and motivations of a particular character. Many are also what are known as 'angst vids', meaning that they explore the torment and anguish of the character. These vids leave out many of the family-friendly or comedic elements of the original source material, and are almost always set to dramatic ballads. The vid 'My skin' by raspberry_splat is typical of this type, which analyses the journey of the Doctor. According to the summary for the vid written by the vidder: 'A damaged Doctor finds, but also loses, much. Sadly his path continues to be one of guilt ridden darkness and loneliness.' This vid intersperses close-up shots of the Doctor's face with scenes of planets exploding, alien races defeated and in particular shows the Daleks, the Doctor's nemeses, the alien race which he is forced to destroy over and over again. This vid explores the Doctor's internal conflict as he must destroy one race (the Daleks) to save another (the humans), and his emotional journey as the last of the Time Lords. Set to a slow, evocative ballad by Natalie Merchant, the video is slowed down dramatically and features slow transitions between shots with long overlays.

In Figure 1, above, the vidder has re-framed the original shot to focus solely on the Doctor's face in close-up to allow the viewer to engage more closely with his expression and emotion. As it is overlaid with an image of Gallifrey, the viewer is given the impression that the Doctor is thinking about his home and his people. All action scenes are removed, and instead the focus is now on the Doctor and the trauma he experiences when having to kill the Daleks, and his loneliness as his companions die or leave him as he continues to live on.

Shots such as Figure 2, above, emphasize the themes of loneliness and separation.

'We're Making Our Own Happy Ending!':
The *Doctor Who* Fan Vidding Community
Katharina Freund

The lyrics and style of the music further reinforce the vidder's particular interpretation as expressed through the vid:

I've been treated so wrong
I've been treated so long
As if I'm becoming untouchable

Contempt loves the silence
It thrives in the dark
With fine winding tendrils
That strangle the heart

They say that promises
Sweeten the blow
But I don't need them
No, I don't need them

Vids like 'My skin' work as a visual summary of a particular theme which occurs throughout the New *Doctor Who* series by bringing together the disparate episodes which feature the Doctor's loneliness and anguish. The music is the connective tissue which ties the clips together into a coherent whole, with the lyrics and style of the piece helping to convey the message intended by the vidder.

Fandom moments
Many vids also draw on popular responses to the text from the fannish community, which are often expressed through posts on LiveJournal and explored through fanfiction. The interpretive fandom of vidding is evident in the highlighting and deconstructing of particular moments within the television text.

Hills notes in his 2008 article on 'moments' in *Doctor Who* fandom that breaking the text down into its component parts is a central practice of *Doctor Who* fandom: 'Fans love to pick out and dwell on textual moments, perhaps more intently and routinely than "casual" audiences.' He continues, 'fans watch for, recall and celebrate or critique what become defining moments within their beloved shows [...] Fans' close readings also tend to *evaluatively break texts into pieces* – greatest bits, rubbish bits, embarrassing bits, scary bits' (original emphasis) This is precisely what occurs when vids are created out of the source text, and vids are often organized around the types of themes that Hills lists (the best scenes, the scary scenes, the embarrassing scenes, and so forth). Hills notes that moments with 'overtly marked performance' are those that usually stand out to fans.

In the *Doctor Who* fandom on LiveJournal, the community's emotional response

Fig. 3: Rose says goodbye to
the Doctor in 'Tabula rasa'.
(@hollywoodgrrl;
Doctor Who ©BBC).

Fig. 4: The Tenth
Doctor in 'Tabula rasa'.
(@hollywoodgrrl;
Doctor Who ©BBC).

Fig. 5: John Smith remembers
Rose. (@hollywoodgrrl;
Doctor Who ©BBC).

to key moments from the series is perhaps best seen in relationship ('shipper') vidders dedicated to the Tenth Doctor and Rose. In the vid 'Tabula rasa' (Latin for 'blank slate'), American vidder hollywoodgrrl explores her emotional response to Episodes 308 ('Human Nature' [Palmer, 2007, Series 3, Episode 8]) and 309 ('The Family of Blood' [Palmer, 2007, Series 3, Episode 9]) in the context of her 'shipping for the Tenth Doctor and Rose. In these episodes, the Doctor is forced to erase his Time Lord identity and hide from 'The Family' disguised as a human named John Smith. He eventually recovers his memories, and suddenly remembers his life as the Doctor. For hollywoodgrrl, though, the most important element for the Doctor to remember was his love of Rose.

This vid highlights those moments of overtly marked performance in the relationship between the Tenth Doctor and Rose by focusing on key scenes, particularly their separation and final goodbye in the Series 2 finale. These scenes are framed by shots of John Smith as he looks into the fob watch containing his Time Lord memories (see Figures 3, 4 and 5). Dramatic music and lines of dialogue from key scenes further reinforce a painful, emotional reading for the vid. In the series itself, despite the heartbreaking goodbye scenes between the Doctor and Rose at the end of Series 2 and the implied profession of love between the characters, many fans felt that the Doctor moved on to another companion too quickly after Billie Piper's exit from the series. For fans of the Doctor/Rose 'ship, this vid addresses that gap by including Rose retroactively in the Doctor's thoughts, and adds depth and poignancy to later episodes which no longer feature their favourite companion. Many viewers of the vid left comments about their affective response by saying that it made them want to cry: rather than being negative, this response is a measure of the vid's quality in evoking feelings in the viewer.

Vidders are simultaneously emotional and critical viewers of television. Jenkins writes about how fannish viewing practices offered a challenge to the traditional notion of media consumption: fans are emotionally engaged with media texts, and experience intense emotional reactions to events in the series that are seen as strange or excessive to non-fans. He does, however, also point out that fans are simultaneously the harshest critics of the television they adore. Purnima Mankekar discusses this contradiction:

Not only do the viewers critique the programmes themselves (the director's work, the

'We're Making Our Own Happy Ending!':
The *Doctor Who* Fan Vidding Community
Katharina Freund

plot, the camera angles) but they can also 'see through' to the political agendas embedded in the story's narrative. And yet, *at the same time*, they find themselves emotionally drawn into the story and its characters, and experience a sense of connectedness to the world.

Similarly, although the vids discussed above are examples of intense emotional interaction with *Doctor Who*, this next type of vid deals with fannish displeasure and tension within the text.

In addition to the 'moments' celebrated in the Doctor vids and the 'shipper vids, the other key type of vid common to *Doctor Who* fandom is the companion tribute. These tribute vids show fannish love for the supporting (and almost always female) characters of the companions. Vidders seek to demonstrate their affection for specific companions who have left the show through vids that showcase the character's achievements in the series.

These types of vids also seek to reclaim or defend how the series treated certain characters. Many vidders described themselves as in conflict with creator Russell T. Davies after Donna's exit at the conclusion of Series 4. According to a vidder from the United Kingdom: '*Doctor Who*, with the Donna storyline [...] there's been quite a few vids that have tried to correct that. We're making our own happy ending for the story, because he [Davies] shouldn't have done that to Donna!'

Despite this vidder's love for the character, she was unable to control the outcome and thus turned to fandom in order to work through her feelings about the Series 4 finale. A plethora of vids appeared at this time which focused on the great feats and adventures that Donna had on the show, and explored how important her character was to that particular season, and also several that sought to re-write what happened to Donna and replace it with a more desirable turn of events.

The vid 'Don't lose yourself' by sweetestdrain is one such example of the fannish response to Donna's exit from *Doctor Who*. It focuses on the relationship between Donna and the Doctor, with scenes from Pompeii, the Library, and the Ood planet set to lyrics of love and adventure as seen in the following clips, to the song of the same name by Laura Veirs (Figures 8.6, 8.7 and 8.8).

We slept in the shadow of a cedar tree
We made love on the rising tide

(Figure 6)

Fig. 8: Shot from 'Don't lose yourself'. (©sweetestdrain; Doctor Who ©BBC).

Fig. 9: The Doctor erases Donna's memory in 'Don't lose yourself'. (©sweetestdrain; Doctor Who ©BBC).

We smelled the perfume of the waxing moon
We dreamt of all the friendships kind

(Figure 7)

We touched the blood of the black cat
We pet the mammoth dog of tears

(Figure 8)

In the flickering light we were laughing
Necessity conquers fear

The latter section of the vid focuses on Donna saving the world, and then having her memory wiped by the Doctor. The lyrics simply repeat 'Don't lose yourself / Don't let yourself be lost / Don't lose yourself' over and over again, as Donna's memories are erased (Figure 8.9).

(Figure 9)

The song ends suddenly and the vid shows a final shot (Figure 10) of the Doctor embracing Donna in silence.

(Figure 10)

It could be argued that the repeated lyric 'Don't lose yourself' is the voice of the fans of the series who were upset with Davies's treatment of Donna in her final episode, and saw it as a particularly cruel development for a character who wanted so badly to have meaning in her life.

Fig. 10: The final shot from 'Don't lose yourself'. (©sweetestdrain; Doctor Who ©BBC).

Conclusion

Through vidding, a specific community of female fans seeks to explore elements of the televisual text that it finds the most engaging. Using their knowledge of television genre conventions and music as highly media-literate fans, vidders demonstrate their own understandings and relationship to the series, and also voice their concerns about developments in the narrative that they found problematic. This reading of *Doctor Who* is not one shared by all fans, but is a product of the community of interpretation found

'We're Making Our Own Happy Ending!':
The *Doctor Who* Fan Vidding Community
Katharina Freund

among the online community of (mostly) female fans in LiveJournal, Tumblr and other
spaces. The examples discussed above show the thoughtful media commentary occurring in the vidding community. This is a specific interpretive community with their own
reading practices, aesthetic styles and concerns. Based on their in-depth knowledge
of television and film traditions and conventions, the vidders are able to make creative
and critical commentary on the media they consume, and exist as artefacts to the emotional viewing experiences of this audience. ●

~~~~~~~~~~~

GO FURTHER

Books

'Veni, Vidi, Vids!': Audiences, Gender and Community in Fan Vidding
Katharina Freund
(Wollongong: University of Wollongong, 2012)

Love and Monsters: The Doctor Who *Experience, 1979 to the Present*
Miles Booy
(London and New York: I.B. Tauris, 2012)

Triumph of a Time Lord: Regenerating Doctor Who *in the Twenty-first Century*
Matt Hills
(London: I.B. Tauris, 2010)

Genre and Television: From Cop Shows to Cartoon in American Culture
Jason Mittell
(New York: Routledge, 2004)

*Screening Culture, Viewing Politics: An Ethnography of Television, Womenhood and
Nation in Postcolonial India*
Purnima Mankekar
(Durham: Duke University Press, 1999)

Textual Poachers: Television Fans and Participatory Culture
Henry Jenkins
(New York: Routledge, 1992)

Unheard Melodies: Narrative Film Music
Claudia Gorbman
(Bloomington: Indiana University Press, 1987)

Extracts/Essays/Articles

'The dispersible television text: Theorising moments of the new *Doctor Who*'
Matt Hills
In *Science Fiction Film and Television*. 1: 1 (2008), pp. 25–44.

Film/Television

Doctor Who [New series], Russell T. Davies, creator (Cardiff, UK: BBC, 2005)

'Human Nature', Charles Palmer, dir. *Doctor Who* [New series] (Cardiff, UK: BBC, 2007)
'Family of Blood', Charles Palmer, dir. *Doctor Who* [New series] (Cardiff, UK: BBC, 2007)

Online
Articles/Essays/Extracts

'Women, *Star Trek*, and the early development of fannish vidding'
Francesca Coppa
In *Transformative Works and Cultures*. 1 (2008), http://journal.transformativeworks.org/index.php/twc/article/view/44

Audio

'Don't lose yourself'
Laura Veirs
Saltbreakers (Warner Bros, 2007)

'My skin'
Natalie Merchant
Ophelia (Elektra, 1997)

Chapter
09

Extermi…Knit!:
Female Fans and Feminine
Handicrafting

Brigid Cherry

→ Much to the delight of one community of *Doctor Who* fans, the Eleventh Doctor revealed himself to be interested in knitting in 'The Impossible Astronaut' (Haynes, 2011, Series 6, Episode 1) and read *Knitting For Girls* magazine in 'The Wedding of River Song' (Webb, 2011, Series 6, Episode 13). It was a significant revelation about the Doctor's personality because these particular fans belong to a community that practises fibre arts and feminine handicrafting.

It is not simply that they knit, crochet or sew as a pastime or practical domestic activity, but also that they do so as a form of fan production – sewing, knitting and crocheting costumes, garments and toys, inspired by and demonstrating their love for *Doctor Who*. The study of handicrafting as a form of female fan production (alongside fanfiction, vidding and costuming/cosplay) represents not only the recognition of a novel form of fan production, but the presentation and sharing of a fan identity. This account looks at the ways in which such identities are constructed within *Doctor Who*-related handicrafting.

Knitting for girls
Within Ravelry, a social networking community dedicated to feminine handicrafting, dedicated fan communities have arisen around texts such as *Lord of the Rings* (Tolkien books published 1954/1955; Jackson films released 2001–03), *Harry Potter* (Rowling, 1997–2007) and *Twilight* (Meyer, 2005–08), as well as *Doctor Who*. This has provided a vibrant arena for the participant-observation of fan handicrafting undertaken for this chapter. Of paramount importance in selecting Ravelry as the focus of the data collection is that it works as a closed and close-knit social space for anyone with an interest in feminine handicrafts. The forum section of Ravelry contains several groups specifically created for the discussion of *Doctor Who*. There are at least 25 groups dedicated to *Doctor Who* and its spin-off *Torchwood* (Davies, BBC, 2006–11). The largest and most active groups are 'Who Knits?' with 6,610 members, 'Dr Who-ites' with 3,238, and 'I Dye For Doctor Who' with 2,257. One of the smaller groups – 'Doctor Who on You', specifically focused on recreating *Doctor Who* costumes (384 members) – was also included in this participant-observation. The *Doctor Who* fan knitters form a community, but they do not only stay within discrete groups. They often take part in communal handicrafting activities involving both wider groupings of fans and the Ravelry community generally. For example, they formed a Team TARDIS in both the Nerd Wars handicrafting challenges and the Ravellenic Games that ran in parallel with the official Olympic Games.

These fans are quite a different community from the one found in *Doctor Who* online fan communities such as Gallifrey Base. Although some fan handicrafters are active participants in other fan communities, this group is more likely to include casual viewers who do not otherwise participate in organized fandom or online *Doctor Who* fan communities. Most had not seen episodes of Classic *Who* (this might change once they joined the group and were introduced to the Classic series by more intense fans) and were specifically attracted to the programme with the reboot, particularly with David Tennant (indeed, many of them could more accurately be classified as David Tennant fans). They may not have the same fan competencies – or even the same levels of interest in *Doctor Who* – as the members of Gallifrey Base. As Henry Jenkins has discussed in *Textual Poachers* (1992), whereas many male fans acquire detailed knowledge about production and other factual information (masculine fan competencies), female fans tend to be more invested in the emotions and relationships within the text (feminine

Extermi...Knit!: Female Fans and Feminine Handicrafting
Brigid Cherry

Fig. 1: A knitted TARDIS toy
and crochet second Doctor.
(©Lotta Groeger; Doctor Who
©BBC).

competencies).

In this case, the social networking offered by Ravelry provides established fans with a niche space where they can discuss their emotional investment in the series without having to feel they lack detailed knowledge, and allows casual or new fans to simply chat with other *Doctor Who* fans and participate in themed knitting without taking on a deeper commitment to fan culture. Communities such as Ravelry allow intense fans and casual viewers to participate within the same groups and on a relatively equal footing around the shared practices of handicrafting. This does not exclude casual viewers or intensely emotional female fans who might not have access to the fanspeak or detailed cultural competencies required in a more intensely fannish forum.

It also allows potential entry into more intense fandom as longer-term or more knowledgeable fans 'initiate' newer or more casual fans into Classic *Who* or other areas of *Who* fandom. For example, NWI[1] (female, 30s, EU, IT) joined Team TARDIS only having watched New *Who* but has subsequently started watching the Classic series: 'It took me some while till I got to watch also some of these. But when I finally did I totally fell for Classic *Who* too.' Second, since the handicrafting community is predominantly female (there are male knitters but they remain a small minority and regardless of the sex of the handicrafters it is often a feminine practice), gendered fan behaviours emerge. The Ravelry forums provide a space for intensely feminine fandom that some male-dominated, masculine fandom groups look down on (feminine fandom is often referred to pejoratively as fangirling or squee). The fan handicrafting groups can be intensely emotional and eroticized. This can be seen in their Ravaters – a large number of which are pictures of Tennant as the Doctor – and the frequent comments and postings of pictures that they can 'squee' over.

A *Doctor Who* pattern book
Aside from such overt displays (which might be seen in any non-handicrafting fan community), how do these fans make use of their handicrafting to demonstrate their fan interests? Within the Ravelry community there are several ways they can do this. As well as typical fan chat and discussion of texts, fans write and craft various patterns, dye yarn in thematic colourways, and take part in communal activities such as knit- and crochet-alongs. Fans choose to create *Doctor Who* handicraft patterns for themselves. There are over 280 *Doctor Who*-themed patterns falling into several categories. The largest are themed non-costume-specific clothing and accessories (79 patterns) and themed household and personal items (77), followed by toys and stuffed crochet figures

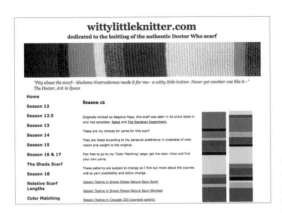

Fig. 2: The WittyLittleKnitter website provides templates for the Fourth Doctor's scarves. (©Tara Carstensen; Doctor Who ©BBC).

commonly known by the Japanese term amigurumi (49) and replica costume items (45). There are also 35 other patterns for knitted or crocheted portraits of characters, clothing for dolls and other items, including charted logos (see Figure 1).

Of the copies of knitted items worn by characters in the series, the most popular is the Fourth Doctor's scarf. There are 27 versions of the scarf listed in the Ravelry pattern database and these reproduce (with some variation) all variants of the scarves worn by Tom Baker on screen. These are as exact as possible, with fans having studied the episodes in which the scarf variants appear and sometimes having inspected the originals in order to create the width and arrangement of stripes for different seasons or even specific episodes (the scarf changed frequently, not only with different scarves being made but existing scarves having sections removed due to fraying or stretching and sections from different scarves being sewn together). The knitting of a scarf can become part of the fan interaction in the Ravelry groups. Knitters can upload an app from *wittylittleknitter.com* to display a progress chart (a picture of the complete scarf) with coloured-in sections to indicate how far they have got. For example, when two members of Team TARDIS in Nerd Wars knitted a scarf for their three-month project (a dissertation) the theme thread displayed their progress so that all the members of the team could offer encouragement and support. This reflects the way in which Nerd Wars and Ravellenic Games teams, as well as various craft-alongs and swaps, facilitate the sociability of fan handicrafting.

Hello, I'm the Doctor

The popularity of the scarf patterns might well be expected, but it does raise an important point about the making and wearing of reproduction costumes. Since the Fourth Doctor's very long scarf is one of the key iconic elements of the programme, this is one of the most worn items for cosplay (Figure 2). Although cosplayers can buy a ready-made scarf from sites like Etsy or an authorized version licensed by the BBC, fans frequently knit their own or commission a friend or family member to knit one for them. The scarf however is part of the costume worn by a male character, but in the main the fan knitters are not making the scarf for male partners, relatives or friends. Many of the fans make it for themselves, and further some make and wear it as part of a *Doctor Who* costume at fan conventions and other events. This suggests a form of cross-gender identification and cross-dressing, or crossplay.

The fact that female fans cosplay the Doctor, however, is not necessarily straightforward. Cosplay is a form of subcultural practice in its own right, particularly in the forms represented within Japanese youth culture. The influence of cosplaying and cosplay events has led to the adoption of the term amongst fan cultures for all costuming practices. Cosplay takes place within social spaces at fan conventions and involves various

Extermi…Knit!: Female Fans and Feminine Handicrafting
Brigid Cherry

degrees of role playing, or 'performative consumption' as Matt Hills calls it in *Fan Cultures* (2002). As he says, this is not necessarily a straightforward form of impersonation in which the self is subsumed in the character. Nor does it always involve identification with or a strong liking for the character being cosplayed. As Nicolle Lamerichs outlines in 'Stranger than fiction' (2011), the reasons for cosplaying particular characters may be complex. Fans may, for example, cosplay a character because they identify with him/her and want to be or at least role play that character for a time, but equally the fan might like the particular costume, or the costume might be one she is able to make within her own level of skills.

Fem!Doctor cosplay is a particular example of *Doctor Who* cosplay in which female fans make feminized versions of the Doctor's various costumes for fan conventions and other cosplay events. Female cosplayers negotiate their liking for a programme with a male lead character by feminizing the clothing associated with that character, thus enabling them to cosplay a character without cross-dressing or blurring their own gender boundaries. This suggests that role play and identification are strong – these female fans are not (or not only) identifying with the main female characters, the companions, but identify as strongly as male fans with the Doctor. But the very act of feminizing the costume also indicates playfulness within the fan culture. NWH (female, 20s, science teacher) says, 'I have female versions of the 4th, 5th, 6th, and 7th Doctors. I am currently working on costumes of the 3rd and 10th Doctors.' She does not however feel that she is totally immersed in the character/fully role plays:

I love all the comments I get while cosplaying. I am too much of a fan girl to stay in character, but I love it when people comment on the quality of my costumes or just to say that they are happy someone is dressed as 'their Doctor'.

Cosplay can of course involve many different forms of crafting, dressmaking, leatherworking, modelling, customizing (with paint, modelling clay, etc.), make-up and prosthetics. It does not depend solely on traditional feminine handicrafts, but combines these with what might be traditionally cast as masculine technology. For example, NWH has not only made a feminized Fourth Doctor costume but has also built an 80 per cent-scale K9 onto the chassis of a remote control car so that it can move about conventions with her.

Fan handicrafters also seek to recreate other knitted items worn by characters in the programme, especially those worn by female companions. This recreation is not just for organized cosplay at fan events and conventions but also allows the fans to incorporate single items into everyday clothing. This demonstrates their love of the programme or a particular character but not necessarily in an overt or 'geeky' way. Indeed, since many of the costume elements that the fan handicrafters recreate are available from high street shops, they can pass as fashionable clothing. For example, Amy's blue-and-white striped

Fig. 3: Fan created knitting chart for making a copy of Amy's jumper. (Doctor Who ©BBC).

jumper from Reiss was seen in 'Dinosaurs On a Spaceship' (Metzstein, 2012, Series 7, Episode 2). This works in conjunction with cosplay, since cosplayers and other fans will often buy the original costume item once they have identified which clothing store it was acquired from (Figure 3).

Cosplayers do not always have to make their own costumes. For example, River Song cosplayers often wear the actual dresses, jackets, skirts, boots, shoes and other items of clothing that were worn on the screen, only to have to customize or build from scratch the items they chose (or cannot afford to buy). Amongst the knitting and crochet patterns written by and available to Ravellers are Rose's mitts, Rose's scarf, Martha's tam, and Amy's scarves and matching mittens. When such costume items appeal to the fans, discussion takes place in the 'Ravelry *Who*' forums on how to recreate the garment or accessory. Fans will take screen caps and study them, working out the stitches and techniques needed to reproduce the patterning. Stores' online catalogues are frequently used since these will provide close-ups and more-easily-visible detailing of the pattern. Fans then work up swatches which can be replicated up to a full size item or write a complete pattern. The fans make use of fashion trends but this can be against the grain of consumerism. In one sense, this illustrates the way fan handicrafters negotiate the tensions inherent in being simultaneously inside and outside the processes of commodification, as Hills proposes. It also illustrates the ways in which knowledge of handicrafting techniques and artistic skills are as, if not more, important than knowledge of the text.

Dye-ing for *Doctor Who*

These competencies also come into play when many of the examples of fan handicrafting overlap with other forms of fan art, as in portraits of characters as seen on deviantART and other online fan art sites, or in the past in print fanzines, and fan-made video remixes seen on YouTube. In fan handicrafting, these are represented in stitchcraft portraits, patterned squares (used as washcloths or afghan squares) and illusion knits, and model-making is represented by amigurumi and other three-dimensional objects. The main distinction between other forms of fan art and fan handicrafting lies in the transferability of the resulting art. A fan can create and devise a pattern for a portrait of the Tenth Doctor and Rose, but rather than standing alone as an admired piece of art created by one fan, in the world of fan handicrafting the art can be passed along as a pattern. Any other fan can recreate the art for herself. Furthermore, the piece will not be a straightforward copy, but will reflect the skills and talents of the maker, the choices of yarn fibres and colours, the end use to which the item is put, and any customization that the fan chooses to make. As Maura Kelly states in 'Knitting as a feminist project?' (2008), handicrafters make many choices that individualize each project. They can also craft any other pattern using specifically

Extermi…Knit!: Female Fans and Feminine Handicrafting
Brigid Cherry

Fig. 4: Laura Isaac's Oncoming Storm wristers are inspired by the design of the Daleks. (©Laura Isaac; Doctor Who ©BBC).

chosen colours of yarn or fibre that evokes or represents aspects of the programme and again display these on their project pages. These are an individual display of fan identity, but this can be communicated easily to other fans by linking their project so that it is displayed in the project database on the main group page or by posting pictures and details in the group threads. Other fans can then comment on the pattern or project and, if they wish, press the 'love' button on the post itself and add the project or pattern to their list of favourites (see Figure 4).

This interaction can bring pleasure to the fans as they see their work being appreciated. NWH says that,

I love it when people comment on my knitting designs. I post my patterns for free because I just want to share my nerd-dom. And I often 'squeee' when I see people post things made from my designs because a little piece of me can't believe how popular my patterns are.

Furthermore, the creative process brings pleasures in its own right. NWI (female, 30s, EU, IT) says, 'Making crochet amigurumis is my biggest joy.' Going on:

Fig. 5: A collection of amigurumi Doctors and companions. (©Hana Jaroňová; Doctor Who ©BBC).

It's creative. I love to see how a bundle of fibre (and some stuffing) grows [into] a character in my hands. It's a great challenge to try to give them the features to look like the character – to find some characteristic features and details and then find out the way how to make it in fibre with crochet hook. I'm often also angry during [the] process because things aren't going as they 'should' (i.e. as I've naively imagined them to be) or when I bump in[to] some problem I have no idea how to solve. But it brings great joy when it come[s] out well or even much better than I've expected.

Fans thus build profiles through their handicrafting and this can contribute to the projection of a fan identity.

As the above examples illustrate, the projects that the fan handicrafters make can also substitute for or supplement the collection of merchandise (Figure 5). RGA (single, 20s, EU, student), for example, owns 'some action figures, some posters and a Dalek cookie cutter' but is especially proud of her own figures which, among the figures of Doctors and companions, several adipose and a scarf, include '10(!) Daleks'. She says, 'I like to craft and I like to craft strange things. I really don't know why I started to craft

all Doctors with at least one companion but I love it so far even if they end up as dust collectors.' Her handicrafting has also been used to acquire further access to older episodes of the programme: 'I swapped most of my Daleks and Adiposes for DVDs of Doctor Who.' This suggest that fan handicrafting in and of itself can, in addition to the pleasures and status it brings the fan within the community, also be a form of fan trade.

The relationship between fan art and commerce is further illustrated by the small businesses that arise within the handicrafting community around the associated crafts of dying and spinning. Fans do not only practise their crafting using commercially available yarn. Some have launched small home-based companies dying yarn in colourways inspired by elements of the series, offering these for sale on sites like Etsy or their own micro-business sites. Some offer the opportunity to join a monthly yarn club in order to receive a surprise colourway once a month. For example, Nerd Girl Yarns offers a Who's Your Doctor yarn club in addition to more than 20 different Doctor Who-inspired colourways that can be dyed on demand. These colourways can be emblematic of the love fans share for the text, focusing on characters and other elements of the text that hold meaning or affect for the fans. For example, Nerd Girl Yarns produces colourways that reflect the Tenth Doctor's suit, the sonic screwdriver, monsters such as the Weeping Angels and the Master. Significantly, the names of the colourways reflect fannish interest in the quotability of dialogue, with names such as Oi, Spaceman and Geronimo! The descriptions also make reference to well-loved elements of the show: the colourway Doctor Donna states, 'Inspired by Doctor Donna this yarn combines my favorite Doctor Who characters, the Tenth Doctor and his companion Donna' (Figure 6).

On one level, this added value declares the dyer's fan identity, but on another it is also one shared communally by her customers in her own group on Ravelry. Here the fans discuss the programme alongside discussion of the yarn. In fact, the yarn itself and the dyer become the object of fannish interest and behaviour. Members of the yarn club discuss upcoming instalments with the dyer, raising expectations and sharing spoilers, and the dyer organizes knit and crochet-alongs and swaps so that customers can show off what they make with her yarns. Such shared love of the text between the dyer and her customers is indicative of the hybrid market environment Sal M. Humphreys discusses in 'The challenges of intellectual property for users of social networking sites' (2008). She states that there is no clear distinction between social and commercial economies as they co-exist in the same space. As she suggests of the social network market, the social matters here as much as the commercial and financial. Furthermore, the social network influences both production and consumption within the fan knitting community. This is a socialized fan marketplace, one that exists outside of the culture industries that see fans as an exploitable market. The dyers and pattern designers are fans

Extermi...Knit!: Female Fans and Feminine Handicrafting
Brigid Cherry

themselves and interact within the fan community as fellow fans as well as customers/producers.

Conclusion

Fan status is a defining characteristic in the sociability of these fan knitters, even when they have no experience of actual fan culture or typical fan competencies (which in any case may be deemed masculine fan traits). The expression of fan interest is orientated around the cultural texts themselves, as well as the handicrafting projects they inspire. Fan knitting is clearly social and can be a form of fan production that extends and re-works the narrative. Fans involve themselves in the creative process by re-mediating and re-writing the text, and fan knitting exists at the heart of an intertextual relationship with the originating text. Though fan knitting cannot really be considered an intensive rewriting of the text, the fans' knitted objects can be directly tied into the text and even tell stories of their own. They certainly represent an intense emotional investment in the narrative. ●

GO FURTHER

Books

Fan Cultures
Matt Hills
(London: Routledge, 2002)

Textual Poachers: Television Fans and Participatory Culture
Henry Jenkins
(London: Routledge, 1992)

Extracts/Essays/Articles

'Knit one, bite one: Vampire fandom, fan production and feminine handicrafts'
Brigid Cherry
In Gareth Schott and Kirstine Moffat (eds). *Fanpires: Audience Consumption of the Modern Vampire* (Washington, DC: New Academia Press, 2011), pp. 137–56.

'Stranger than fiction: Fan identity in cosplay'
Nicolle Lamerichs
In *Transformative Works and Cultures*. 7 (2011), doi:10.3983/twc.2011.0246.

Film/Television

Torchwood, Russell T. Davies, creator (Cardiff, UK: BBC, 2006)
Doctor Who [New series], Russell T. Davies, creator (Cardiff, UK: BBC, 2005)

The Impossible Astronaut', Toby Haynes, dir. *Doctor Who* [New series] (Cardiff, UK: BBC, 2011)
The Wedding of River Song', Jeremy Webb, dir. *Doctor Who* [New series] (Cardiff, UK: BBC, 2011)
'Dinosaurs On a Spaceship', Saul Metzstein, dir. *Doctor Who* [New series] (Cardiff, UK: BBC, 2012)

Online
Extracts/Essays/Articles

'How well do you know *Doctor Who*?'
Gavin Fuller
The Telegraph. 21 September 2012, http://www.telegraph.co.uk/culture/tvandradio/doctor-who/9557580/Quiz-how-well-do-you-know-Doctor-Who.html

'Knitting as a feminist project? Untangling the contradictions of the new knitting movement'
Maura Kelly
In *Proceedings of the American Sociological Association Annual Meeting*. 31 July 2008, http://www.allacademic.com/meta/p241231_index.html.

'The challenges of intellectual property for users of social networking sites:
A case study of Ravelry'
Sal M. Humphreys
In *Proceedings Mind Trek*. 7–8 October 2008, http://eprints.qut.edu.au/14858/.

Websites

Nerd Girl Yarns, http://shop.nerdgirlyarns.com/
Ravelry, http://www.ravelry.com/
Witty Little Knitter, wittylittleknitter.com

Notes
1. Participants in the study are referred to by a code to identify the group they come from (NW = Nerd Wars, RG = Ravellenic Games) followed by the initial of their online name.

Chapter
10

The Language(s)
of Gallifrey

Denise Vultee

→ **What does the language section of CAL's Library look like? What alphabet did Apalapucia use in its travel brochures? How does the speech of Clom really sound, and is it a dialect of Raxacoricofallapatorian?**

These are questions that remain unanswered – and, come to that, unasked – in the *Doctor Who* canon. Although intelligent alien life forms play a central role in virtually every episode of the series, viewers have rarely heard or seen the languages of these alien species. According to the show's premise, the Doctor and his companions in the TARDIS can converse effortlessly with everyone from ancient Romans to Sontarans. The rare exceptions – the rhyming monosyllables of the Judoon in 'Smith and Jones' (Palmer, 2007, Series 3, Episode 1) and 'The Stolen Earth' (Harper, 2008, Series 4, Episode 12), the insect-like clicking of the Tritovores in 'Planet of the Dead' (Strong, 2009, Specials, Episode 2), the bardic cadences of Ancient North Martian in 'The Waters of Mars' (Harper, 2009, Specials, Episode 3) – only underscore the rule: whatever species the Doctor meets in his travels through time and space, his English-speaking companions (and BBC viewers) will have no trouble understanding it.

Ironically, the most glaring exceptions to this rule are the written versions of the Doctor's native language. As River Song explains in 'A Good Man Goes to War' (Hoar, 2011, Series 6, Episode 7), the TARDIS does not translate Gallifreyan; so, although the Time Lords of Gallifrey deliver their lines in English in 'The End of Time' (Lyn, 2010, Specials, Episodes 4&5) and numerous episodes of the Classic series, viewers see written Gallifreyan depicted in an alien script – or, rather, in one of the several distinct scripts that have appeared on the show over the years.

These brief, tantalizing glimpses of written Gallifreyan suggest the tip of a linguistic iceberg, but one that the show's writers have never fully mapped. In some fan communities, constructed languages (or 'conlangs') are part of the canon: *Lord of the Rings* (Tolkien, 1954/1955) fans can refer to Tolkien's appendices to settle wagers over Elvish; Trekkers defer to the authority of linguist Marc Okrand, who created the Klingon language. These are just the best-known examples; on the website *io9: We come from the future*, Alasdair Wilkins has compiled a list of '13 alien languages you can actually read' (2009). But Gallifreyan is not among them. There is no complete BBC-sanctioned version of any Gallifreyan writing system. Partly for this reason, and partly because social media have made it easier for Whovians (and non-Whovians) around the globe to collaborate, many in the *Doctor Who* fan community and beyond have taken matters into their own hands. Together, they have constructed a rich variety of Gallifreyan alphabets, fonts, dictionaries, tutorials and other resources. These resources, in turn, have inspired a growing community of fan artists in their own creative endeavours.

This chapter begins with a brief survey of the three main forms of written Gallifreyan that have appeared in the *Doctor Who* TV series over the years, then goes on to explore fans' efforts to reconstruct and disseminate their own versions of the language, emphasizing the role of social media in facilitating creative collaborations among artists in the *Doctor Who* fan community and beyond who share a fascination with the languages of Gallifrey.

BBC-made versions of Gallifreyan
Written forms of Gallifreyan appeared sporadically in the Classic BBC series beginning

The Language(s) of Gallifrey
Denise Vultee

Fig. 1: Old High Gallifreyan
inscription from the Tomb of
Rasillon, in The Five Doctors
(1983). (Doctor Who ©BBC).

Fig. 2: 'Hello Sweetie' in
Old High Gallifreyan, from
'The Time of Angels' (2010).
(Doctor Who ©BBC).

as early as the 1970s. Even within the context of the show, continuity doesn't seem to have been a priority; in the early days, no two forms of Gallifreyan looked exactly alike. Isolated inscriptions or notes showed up briefly, years or even decades apart. Broadly speaking, however, Gallifreyan writing can be divided into three types: Old High, modern and circular.

Old High Gallifreyan (OHG) was the language of Rassilon, founder of the Time Lords; several different versions have appeared on the show and in authorized publications. The OHG inscription from the tomb of Rassilon in *The Five Doctors* (Moffatt, 1983, Special) combines Greek letters, numerals, arrows and mathematical symbols (Figure 1).

In New *Who*, OHG has reappeared as River Song's language of choice in the graffiti she uses to get the Doctor's attention. In 'The Time of Angels' (Smith, 2010, Series 5, Episode 4), the Eleventh Doctor waxes nostalgic over a museum artefact etched with OHG: 'The lost language of the Time Lords. There were days [...] these words could burn stars, and raise up empires, and topple gods.' These particular words, however, turn out to be River's signature line: 'Hello, Sweetie' (Figure 2).

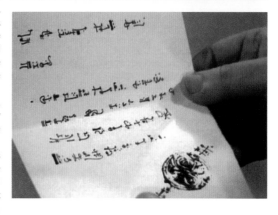

In a later episode, 'The Pandorica Opens' (Haynes, 2010, Series 5, Episode 12), River Song summons the Doctor by defacing the oldest writing in the universe with a message of her own, supplying her space-time coordinates in OHG.

By the Doctor's time, the language of Rassilon was largely forgotten; it took several of his 'selves' in *The Five Doctors* to make sense of the inscription. A more fluid script, often called 'modern Gallifreyan' to differentiate it from OHG, took its place. Modern Gallifreyan handwriting has appeared only rarely on the show, most memorably in a warning note handwritten by the Fourth Doctor in *The Deadly Assassin* (Maloney, 1976, Season 14, Figure 3).

Fig. 3: The Fourth Doctor's
warning note in modern
Gallifreyan, from The
Deadly Assassin (1976).
(Doctor Who ©BBC).

When the series returned to production in 2005, both the interior of the TARDIS and the Gallifreyan writing system had a new look. Circular Gallifreyan – a complex system of interlocking circles, semicircles and lines – is in many ways a combination of the mundane and the exotic. On the one hand, it is apparently the Doctor's everyday working language, showing up on everything from the Tenth Doctor's ubiquitous yellow sticky notes to the Eleventh Doctor's updated console décor in New *Who* Series 7. But on the other hand, it also has an air of mystery and antiquity about it, as in the scene

Fig. 4: The Visionary, surrounded by circular Gallifreyan, from 'The End of Time' (2010). (Doctor Who ©BBC).

Fig. 5: The Doctor's cot, from 'A Good Man Goes to War' (2011). (Doctor Who ©BBC).

from 'The End of Time' in which the Visionary scrawls her prophecies (Figure 4).

And it plays a pivotal role in revealing River Song's true identity in 'A Good Man Goes to War', where it decorates the side of the Doctor's cot (Figure 5).

In addition to the TV series, the *Doctor Who* New Series Adventures, published by BBC Books, have also featured examples of circular Gallifreyan – most notably on the spines and behind the chapter numbers of the Ninth and Tenth Doctor novels, where they were arranged to suggest a base-7 numbering system. It's unclear whether circular script represents a particular version of Gallifreyan, or whether it is perhaps a hybrid system, like Chinese ideograms or Tolkien's Tengwar script, that can be adapted to write multiple languages.

Fan-made versions of Gallifreyan

The fragments of Gallifreyan that have appeared over the past half-century have piqued fans' interest while leaving enormous scope for invention. What Robert V. Kozinets observed about *Star Trek* (Roddenberry, CBS, 1966–69) in his 2007 article 'Inno-tribes: *Star Trek* as wikimedia' is also true of *Doctor Who*: the complexity of the show's world, coupled with the diversity of its fans' interests and talents, has sparked a flourishing culture of creative appropriation.

Despite the scarcity of canonical material, fans have worked to wrestle both OHG and modern Gallifreyan into coherent systems. These two forms of writing are sometimes categorized as 'linear Gallifreyan' to distinguish them from circular. In his article 'Old High Gallifreyan', which appeared originally in the October 1994 issue of the New Zealand fanzine *TSV*, Jon Preddle provided handwritten images of the linear forms of Gallifreyan that had appeared in the Classic series through 1989 (and in the home video version of *Shada* (Roberts, 1980, Season 17), released in 1992). More recently, using Preddle's article and other web resources, the author of the Tumblr blogs *Freakism* and *Odd things happen* has constructed a phonetic alphabet (or 'omegabet', to borrow Lance's Parkin's term from the novel *Doctor Who: The Gallifrey Chronicles* [2005]) for OHG. As of this writing, the system consists of 41 symbols, corresponding to 19 vowels and 22 consonants in the International Phonetic Alphabet (IPA) (Figure 6).

Fonts inspired by linear Gallifreyan have also appeared online, including 'Archaic Gallifreyan' (OHG) and 'Assassin's Gallifreyan' (modern Gallifreyan), both on the social font-sharing website FontStruct. The claim, repeated without attribution on many fan websites, that OHG had ten million characters and modern Gallifreyan 'only' one million, doesn't appear to have deterred such projects.

The Language(s) of Gallifrey
Denise Vultee

OLD HIGH GALLIFREYAN

The symbol on the left of each column is the International Phonetic Alphabet symbol.
The letters are pronounced the same as the underlined Earth English letter.
The Gallifreyan symbol is written on the right.

Vowels

IPA	Word	Symbol
ɑː	arm	
æ	cat	
e	met	
ə	away	
ɜːʳ	turn	
ɪ	hit	
iː	see	
ɒ	hot	
ʊ	put	
uː	too	
aɪ	five	
aʊ	now	
eɪ	say	
j	yes	
oʊ	go	
ɔɪ	boy	
eəʳ	where	
ɪəʳ	near	
ʊəʳ	pure	

Consonants

IPA	Word	Symbol
b	lab	
d	did	
f	find	
g	give	
h	how	
k	cat	
l	leg	
m	lemon	
n	no	
ŋ	sing	
p	pet	
r	red	
s	sun	
ʃ	she	
t	tea	
tʃ	check	
θ	think	
v	voice	
w	wet	
z	zoo	
ʒ	pleasure	
dʒ	just	

With thanks to: http://tinyurl.com/intphoalp
for providing the IPA examples and symbols
I used here.

www.lubol.tumblr.com
There's none of that infringement intended, just one sad guy trying to get something free
unto the world

Fig. 6 (opposite): Old High
Gallifreyan alphabet, from
'Odd things happen' blog
on Tumblr. (©odd-things-
happen.tumblr.com; Doctor
Who ©BBC).

But the version of the language that seems to have captured the imagination of fans most thoroughly since its appearance in 2005 is circular Gallifreyan. A simple explanation for this phenomenon is that, like bowties and fezzes, 'circular is cool'. One blogger makes just this point in 'Learn Gallifreyan in 13 easy timelines' (2012), a post on the *Fandom entanglement* blog that provides a useful overview of the varieties of Gallifreyan available online. Beyond its inherent aesthetic appeal, however, the popularity of circular Gallifreyan may also owe something to the fact that its debut in New *Who* coincided with the rise of social media venues that facilitate sharing and collaboration in the graphic arts.

Two websites in particular – Tumblr and deviantART – have been instrumental in creating communities around circular Gallifreyan. In addition to artworks, members of both these communities create and share educational resources, such as circular Gallifreyan tutorials, and technical resources, such as graphics software to aid in drawing the circular script. The majority of circular Gallifreyan tutorials on the Internet have been created by English speakers to provide a systematic way of rendering English words and phrases into shapes that resemble the circular script seen on the show. In some systems of circular Gallifreyan, however, the shapes correspond to ideas rather than to English letters or sounds. And while circular Gallifreyan may not seem a likely candidate for a typeface, a version called 'WS simple Gallifreyan font' is available on the font-sharing sites Dafont and Font River.

The online activity surrounding circular Gallifreyan shares some features of patterns researchers have observed in other online creative communities. In their 2012 article 'Teen content creators: Experiences of using information to learn', Mary Ann Harlan and her colleagues at Queensland University of Technology identified four stages of online 'creating practices' – *participating*, *copying*, *modelling* and *composing* – that provide useful categories for understanding how fans collaborate on social media to produce the rich varieties of circular Gallifreyan writing systems described below, as well as the creative projects these systems inspire.

Participating is, of course, a basic activity for members of any online community; it includes behaviours such as commenting on and/or rating the contributions of other members. In the communities that have formed around circular Gallifreyan, commenters often praise the originality or beauty of a design; faithfulness to the versions seen on the TV series seems to be optional. One artist summed up this attitude concisely: 'No, it's not canon. But it is beautiful.' Nevertheless, faithfulness to the spirit, if not the letter, of the show is also honoured: for example, one deviantART commenter remarked, 'The fact that I had to check your note to find out if this was copied directly off *Dr. Who* or your own creation is a credit to your work!' Those artists who create their own systems (such as those described below), rather than copying or modelling others' designs, are held in particularly high esteem. Commenters often ask where an artist 'learned' Gallifreyan; and if the answer is some variant of 'I made it up myself', the reaction is typi-

The Language(s) of Gallifrey
Denise Vultee

cally one of awe. While many online comments about circular Gallifreyan simply express admiration for the artist's talents, others reveal a high level of expertise; indeed, community members often point out 'errors' in the efforts of those at the modelling stage, described below, to combine the elements of widely adopted systems into words and phrases.

Copying is an unglamorous but necessary practice, particularly for visual artists, who use it to achieve technical competence. Widely shared images from both the TV series and the fan-made systems of circular Gallifreyan provide ample material for fans who are at this stage in their work. A good example of copying can be seen in the numerous attempts to accurately reproduce the design from the cot in 'A Good Man Goes to War'. Once these copied designs are shared on social media, however, they tend to take on a life of their own, as artists combine them with other shared resources such as Photoshop brushes to create new works, while others borrow them for use in everyday items such as T-shirts and iPhone backgrounds.

Modelling is one step removed from copying, but it also involves learning by example; in this stage, the works of others serve as a source of inspiration, but the artist rearranges or alters their elements. Hybrid systems of circular Gallifreyan (such as those of Loren Sherman or the Gallifreyan Conlang Project, described below), in which each symbol corresponds to an English letter or sound, allow users to personalize designs by transcribing their own names or those of their loved ones into aesthetically pleasing objects. Some of these systems are quite flexible, with multiple 'correct' ways to construct a given word. Several Tumblr blogs are entirely devoted to circular Gallifreyan script, including *Written in Gallifrey*, *Catherine writes Gallifreyan*, *I write in Gallifreyan* and *Gallifreyan Who quotes* (which specializes in transcribing dialogue from the TV show). Collaboration across media is the order of the day: one jewellery maker shared a photo of the wire pendant she had designed using another Tumblr member's circular Gallifreyan version of the name 'Sherlock Holmes'. Artists who display skill in modelling often receive special requests from other community members who want to see their names or favourite phrases 'translated' into Gallifreyan.

One frequent question wherever circular Gallifreyan appears on social media sites is, 'Can I use your design as a tattoo?' The motivation to acquire such a tattoo may be straightforward or complex. The shapes themselves are aesthetically appealing, apart from any meaning that might be attached to them; and dedicated fans of all stripes, from football to pop music, often choose body art that reflects their self-identification. But the lure of circular Gallifreyan probably owes something as well to the strong interest, in western society since the 1980s, in body art that incorporates symbols borrowed from ancient and non-western cultures. Gallifrey, after all, is arguably as ancient a culture as one could wish for. And Time Lords themselves were known to sport tattoos: we get a glimpse of the Third Doctor's in *Spearhead from Space* (Martinus, 1970, Season 7), and an ouroboros tattoo allows the Eleventh Doctor to identify the arm of his friend

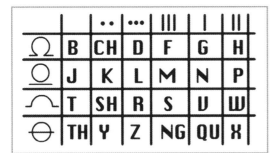

		..	...	|||			||
Ω	B	CH	D	F	G	H
O	J	K	L	M	N	P
⌒	T	SH	R	S	U	W
⊖	TH	Y	Z	NG	QU	X

Fig. 7: Consonant chart for Loren Sherman's circular Gallifreyan system, from Sherman's Planet. (©www.shermansplanet.com/gallifreyan; Doctor Who ©BBC).

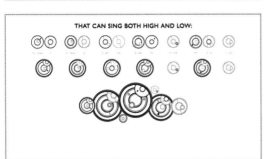

THAT CAN SING BOTH HIGH AND LOW:

Fig. 8: 'That can sing both high and low' (a line from Shakespeare's poem 'O mistress mine' from Twelfth Night) in 'Doctor's cot Gallifreyan', (©Brittany Goodman, brittanybgood tumblr.com; Doctor Who ©BBC).

the Corsair in 'The Doctor's Wife' (Clark, 2011, Series 6, Episode 4). Moreover, borrowing symbols from a fictional culture such as Gallifrey can allay the discomfort Margo DeMello describes, in her 2000 book *Bodies of Inscription: A Cultural History of the Modern Tattoo Community*, as a side-effect of appropriating non-western symbols for display on western bodies.

The modelling stage, whether it takes the form of commitment to an ongoing blog or the permanence of body art, suggests a deep level of involvement with a fan community. A few fans take their expertise to the next level: *composing*, an advanced creative practice in which, according to Harlan and her colleagues, members of a community apply their acquired knowledge to create something new. In the context of circular Gallifreyan, this can mean creating an original writing system – or even an entire language – with its own complex set of rules.

One of the more popular circular Gallifreyan alphabets was created by Loren Sherman in 2011, based on an earlier version by Catherine Bettenbender. It consists of a combination of circles, divots, lines and dots representing letters of the English alphabet, along with rules for arranging and attaching them to form words and sentences (Figure 7).

Words are formed by writing the first letter at the bottom of a circle and proceeding anticlockwise. A sentence is a larger circle comprising a collection of words, also arranged anticlockwise. In addition to letters, Sherman's system includes numbers and a guide for writing mathematical equations. Full instructions for writing with this system can be found on the website *Sherman's planet*; another user has posted simplified rules under 'Circular Gallifreyan' on the 'Time turners of the T.A.R.D.I.S. wiki' (2012).

Inspired by Sherman's lead but taking a different direction, graphic artist BrittanyB-Good [online name] designed a version of circular Gallifreyan called 'Doctor's Cot Gallifreyan', a phonetic system based on the collection of concentric circles that appears on the side of the Doctor's crib in 'A Good Man Goes to War'. Each consonant-vowel pair is represented by a circle consisting of three parts (an outer circle, an inner circle, and the open space between them). A word is formed by enclosing several of these pairs within a single circle; a sentence is a series of overlapping circles of various sizes, arranged from left to right (Figure 8).

The most ambitious phonetic version of the language to date is Collective Gallifreyan, constructed by the members of the Gallifreyan Conlang Project (Figure 9). This collaborative effort, started by linguistics student Tamara Fritz, was still in progress as of this writing, with more than 20 active contributors. Their stated goal is to create a full-blown constructed Gallifreyan language, complete with its own alphabet, vocabulary

The Language(s) of Gallifrey
Denise Vultee

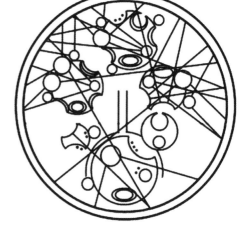

Fig. 9: Sample sentence in Collective Gallifreyan: 'Gormi' Uθ Nεçpɑn Gɑlifrɛjli Klɑsɛjçil dɪz *['Hello' from The Gallifreyan Conlang Project]. (©Brooke Schalow of the Gallifreyan Conlang Project, creatinggallifreyan.tumblr. com; Doctor Who ©BBC).*

and grammar. Resources available on the project's website include an alphabet book, a Gallifreyan-English dictionary, a guide to grammar and a Gallifreyan IPA keyboard.

Not all fan-made circular Gallifreyan is alphabetical or phonetic. Some is ideographic – that is, based on the meanings of words rather than on their pronunciation. One example, created as a design exercise by DrawlingNell [online name] on deviantART, uses polygons, ellipses and other shapes as well as circles to create a select vocabulary of nouns, pronouns and adjectives, many of which relate thematically to the TV series (e.g. 'vortex', 'space', 'sonic'). Some of these figures create the illusion of three-dimensionality, while others appear two-dimensional; some pairs, such 'lord' and 'lady' or 'ascent' and 'descent', have contrasting elements that mark them as opposites; some have shapes that suggest their meanings (e.g. a busy collection of nested circles and polygons for 'confusion'), while for others the connection between form and definition is more mysterious.

Another concept-based variant of circular Gallifreyan was created by Greencrook, also known as LewisCrook [online names], who has shared his work on both deviantART and Tumblr. He has written a grammar and dictionary for this system, which uses a complex and visually elegant combination of circles, curves and links to construct whole sentences, complete with variations for verb tenses and moods. His system embraces ambiguity, and the composition and interpretation of texts (according to his grammar guide) often depend more on situational factors than on hard-and-fast rules.

Through all these encounters with the Gallifreyan language, fans have taken what may well be the Doctor's most visibly alien feature and made it their own. They have sorted through the scattered remnants of his language and, together, made them into a mosaic that is greater than the sum of the fragments. They have spread it around the world, coaxed it into learning their names, and even inscribed it on their bodies. And, as with the Doctor himself, while it's impossible to predict where these fan-made versions of Gallifreyan might be heading next, or what they might look like when they arrive, one thing is certain: it's going to be an interesting journey. ●

GO FURTHER

Books

Doctor Who: The Gallifrey Chronicles
Lance Parkin
(London: BBC Books, 2005)

In the Land of Invented Languages: Esperanto Rock Stars, Klingon Poets, Loglan Lovers, and the Mad Dreamers Who Tried to Build a Perfect Language
Arika Okrent
(New York: Spiegel & Grau, 2009)

Bodies of Inscription: A Cultural History of the Modern Tattoo Community
Margo DeMello
(Durham: Duke University Press, 2000)

Extracts/Essays/Articles

'Teen content creators: Experiences of using information to learn'
Mary Ann Harlan, Christine Bruce and Mandy Lupton
In *Library Trends*. 60:3 (2012), pp. 569–87.

'Inno-tribes: *Star Trek* as wikimedia'
Robert V. Kozinets
In Bernard Cova, Robert V. Kozinets and Avi Shankar (eds). *Consumer Tribes* (Oxford: Elsevier/Butterworth-Heinemann, 2007), pp. 194–211.

Film/Television

Star Trek, Gene Roddenberry, creator (Hollywood, CA: CBS, 1966)
Doctor Who [Classic series], Sydney Newman and Verity Lambert, creators (London, UK: BBC, 1963); [New series], Russell T. Davies, creator (Cardiff, UK: BBC, 2005)

'A Good Man Goes to War', Peter Hoar, dir. *Doctor Who* [New series] (Cardiff, UK: BBC, 2011)
'The Doctor's Wife', Richard Clark, dir. *Doctor Who* [New series] (Cardiff, UK: BBC, 2011)
'The Time of Angels', Adam Smith, dir. *Doctor Who* [New series] (Cardiff, UK: BBC, 2010)
'The Pandorica Opens', Toby Haynes, dir. *Doctor Who* [New series] (Cardiff, UK: BBC, 2010)
'The End of Time', Euros Lyn, dir. *Doctor Who* [New series] (Cardiff, UK: BBC, 2010)
'The Waters of Mars', Graeme Harper, dir. *Doctor Who* [New series] (Cardiff, UK: BBC, 2009)
'Planet of the Dead', James Strong, dir. *Doctor Who* [New series] (Cardiff, UK: BBC, 2009)
'The Stolen Earth', Graeme Harper, dir. *Doctor Who* [New series] (Cardiff, UK: BBC, 2008)
'Smith and Jones', Charles Palmer, dir. *Doctor Who* [New series] (Cardiff, UK: BBC, 2007)
The Five Doctors, Peter Moffatt, dir. *Doctor Who* [Classic series] (London, UK: BBC, 1983)
Shada, Pennant Roberts, dir. *Doctor Who* [Classic series] (Cardiff, UK: BBC, 1980)
The Deadly Assassin, David Maloney, dir. *Doctor Who* [Classic series] (London, UK: BBC, 1976)
Spearhead from Space, Derek Martinus, dir. *Doctor Who* [Classic series] (London, UK: BBC, 1970)

The Language(s) of Gallifrey
Denise Vultee

**Online
Extracts/Essays/Articles**

'13 alien languages you can actually read'
Alasdair Wilkins
io9. 19 April 2009, http://io9.com/5218119/13-alien-languages-you-can-actually-read

Websites

Doctor Who *DW*, www.bbc.co.uk/programmes/b006q2x0
Sherman's planet, www.shermansplanet.com
Time turners of the T.A.R.D.I.S. wiki, timeturners.wikidot.com/circular-gallifreyan
New Zealand Doctor Who *Fan Club*, nzdwfc.tetrap.com/archive/tsv41/oldhighgalli-freyan.html
deviantART, www.deviantart.com
Tumblr, www.tumblr.com

~~~~~~~

SMART BUNCH TIME LORDS, NO DRESS SENSE, DREADFUL HATS, BUT SMART.

~~~~~~~

THE 11TH DOCTOR
JOURNEY TO THE CENTRE OF THE TARDIS

Chapter
11

'Doctor Who Unbound', the Alternate History and the Fannish Text

Karen Hellekson

→ The literary genre of alternate history posits 'what if' scenarios: what if the South won the Civil War? What if the Nazis occupied Britain during World War II? What if computers were created in the Victorian era? These thought experiments, known in the field of history as counterfactuals, demonstrate the importance of cause and effect – that is, a line linking past and present where an event has repercussions in the future. Alternate history literature, associated with science fiction in part because so many genre authors write it, amplifies these chains of causality.

Yet of course alternate history is not limited to real historical events. The sprawling *Doctor Who* universe has its own series of alternate histories: the *Doctor Who* Unbound series, a range of six stand-alone audio dramas released by Big Finish in 2003, with two sequel titles released in 2005 and 2008. Each of the eight releases posits a 'what if' designed to skew canonical elements from the *Who* universe and provide sometimes shocking insight into the Doctor's psyche. These 'what ifs' include: what if the Sixth Doctor had lost his trial? What if the Doctor and Susan had never left Gallifrey? What if the television programme *Doctor Who* had never been made?

These 'what ifs' require a departure from canon, the authoritative, official text that aired. Certainly the audios can be listened to by someone completely unaware of the *Doctor Who* universe and can be enjoyed simply as entertaining text, with stand-alone stories and narrative arcs. But as with all alternate histories, part of the fun is identifying the changed moment. In-the-know listeners of the audio dramas seek to identify that changed moment, and they revel in their superior knowledge of what is supposed to be. The listener's subject position is that of informed reader. Alternate history as a genre suggests that impersonal historical and social forces may be bent by a single person – that is to say, that individuals have agency, or the power to affect or bring about events. Similarly, *Doctor Who* has always valorized agency, and *Doctor Who* fans have demonstrated agency with their own alternate read on the text. With the Doctor's deep, often firsthand knowledge of the universe and its denizens, his awareness of future events and his superior technology, he is uniquely positioned to do what doctors do best: fix things.

The *Doctor Who* Unbound titles fit within, and even critique, this larger worldview. The pleasure of the Unbound series also works on another level: the audio dramas valorize deep knowledge of the *Doctor Who* universe. This deep knowledge is one hallmark of fans, who organize themselves into groups according to their interests, thus creating a fandom. Fandoms are not monolithic: in the case of *Doctor Who*, there may be fans of the Classic series, the 2005 New *Who* version of the programme, particular Doctors, novels, companions, spin-off characters, audios and so on. All of this is placed under the umbrella of *Doctor Who* fandom, yet the groups may have different fannish practices and may not even be aware of each other. What they do have in common is a deep knowledge of their chosen milieu, which may be reinforced by creating fan projects such as informational wikis, archives that house fanfiction, and forums or other sites where they can talk about what they love. They may also create or consume artworks that they share with each other: stories, poems, manipulated images, videos.

Although the Unbound texts are professionally created under licence from the BBC, they share much in common with fanfiction, those unofficial, unsanctioned stories written by fans using the situations and characters from a media source and shared online. Like fanfiction, the audios are derivative texts written for a specialist audience,

'Doctor Who Unbound', the Alternate History and the Fannish Text
Karen Hellekson

and many of the professional writers and production personnel who work on *Doctor Who* started out as fans but are now producers and creators. The Unbound series may usefully be read in terms of fan practice when it comes to negotiating the canonical source in relationship to the derivative text. The Unbound audio dramas require a deep understanding of the canonical text to be fully explicable. In the interplay of text, canon and reader, the audio dramas require and reward specialist – one might even say fannish – knowledge and reading strategies.

The Unbound audios
The original six 2003 Unbound releases each posit a different 'what if' scenario (Table 1). The two sequels have much in common with their antecedents, so the sequels may be treated together with the original. Only one release, the fifth, 'Deadline' (Briggs, 2003), is not directly set within the *Doctor Who* milieu. The Unbound series can be divided into three groupings according to theme, which revolve around the Doctor's inherent nature: helpful and good in a tight spot, the same as that seen in canon; a passive, rather than active, genius; and as actually evil. These groupings provide a useful structure for essentializing some of the concerns inherent in the texts.

Three of the Unbound series are adventure stories in the Classic *Doctor Who* style. These include 'Sympathy for the Devil' (Russell, 2003) and its sequel, 'Masters of War' (Haigh-Ellery, 2008), as well as 'Exile' (Briggs, 2003). These three audios all riff on the Third Doctor's genesis after the Second Doctor's final adventure, *The War Games* (Maloney, 1969, Season 6). In canon, the Doctor was exiled to Earth, his TARDIS disabled, and his memory altered so he could not repair it. In the Unbound audios, he regenerates differently (in 'Exile', he regenerates into a woman) and ends up elsewhere. These audio releases retain the fundamental nature of the Doctor as someone who helps others and attempts to solve problems. In contrast are the audios that present the Doctor as passive. In 'Auld Mortality' (Briggs, 2003) and its sequel, 'A Storm of Angels' (Ainsworth, 2008), which are explications of the creative process, the Doctor never left Gallifrey; he is now an eccentric old novelist. The Doctor is not a doer but a dreamer. Instead of actually going on adventures, he creates them virtually. These audio dramas are metatexts for the impulse to create *Doctor Who*. The single audio drama set outside the *Doctor Who* universe is 'Deadline', in which a former TV writer, the stand-in for the Doctor, wonders what his life would have been like if that TV show he'd been working on, *Doctor Who*, had ever made it into production. 'Deadline' is about a passive failed creative genius, not the rich, generative one in the other two audios. These audios, with their focus on creativity and storytelling, self-reflexively nod to the (fan) writers themselves. The writer becomes the genius; the audio drama becomes the densely allusive metatext.

'Full Fathom Five' (Haigh-Ellery, 2003) and 'He Jests at Scars' (Russell, 2003) feature radically different Doctors and have dark endings. In the former, the Doctor's changed character is the story's 'what if'. The Doctor is ready to lie and kill to ensure that a hor-

Fig. 1: Big Finish's 'He Jests
at Scars', from the Unbound
series. (©Big Finish).

rible secret remains concealed. Listeners can only agree with this decision, but the methods the Doctor chooses to ensure this outcome are shocking. 'He Jests at Scars' features not the Doctor but the Valeyard (Michael Jayston reprising his role), the villain in the canonical *Trial of a Time Lord* (Mallett/Jones/Clough, 1986, Season 23) sequence. The 'what if' here is that the Sixth Doctor did not triumph at his rigged trial. Now, years later, his companion, Melanie Bush (Bonnie Langford), hopes to find him so she can get the Doctor back, in part by appealing to the Valeyard's better nature – that aspect of him that is, or once was, the Doctor. She is unable to fulfil her quest; instead, she herself is trapped forever. Although each of the Unbound audios deserves in-depth analysis, I now turn to a case study of 'He Jests at Scars', which I've chosen because it is particularly dense in terms of canonicity and requires particularly fannish knowledge to decode, as it densely references not only canonical *Doctor Who* events but also events and characters from spin-offs, texts that fans would know (Figure 1).

A fabulous contradiction

In 'He Jests at Scars', the Doctor is the alternate of an alternate: in canon, the Valeyard is an alternate Doctor, a distillation of his evil side, given life 'somewhere between the Doctor's twelfth and final incarnations', as the Master proclaims in the final episode of the *Trial of a Time Lord* serial, 'The Ultimate Foe' (Clough, 1986, Season 23). Further, in canon, what is real and what is alternate illusion is hard to parse. During the Doctor's trial for interference, the prosecutor, the Valeyard, shows him images that purport to prove his guilt, and the Doctor shows images in his own defence. These images comprise the four adventure stories that make up the *Trial* serial. As viewers come to learn over the course of the serial, the images have been altered, reconfigured, and edited to ensure that the Doctor will be found guilty in a plot hatched by the Master, who has breached the Time Lords' supercomputer, the Matrix. The Doctor fights to reconcile these alternative, deliberately misleading images with the reality that would find him innocent. Further, 'The Ultimate Foe' has a trick ending: when the Doctor escapes the Matrix and its created alternate worlds into the courtroom, he actually didn't; he remained in the Matrix. The climactic episode thus doubles realities. 'He Jests at Scars' plays with this idea of alternative otherness – and implicitly truth versus falsehood – in its very setting. This Unbound release is set (as is eventually discovered) in the Valeyard's TARDIS, so it could be that none of this is true, or none of it happened, or all of it was manipulated, much like the Unbound episode itself. Even Mel is an alternative version of herself, though plausibly so: she is older, bitter, more willing to do whatever it takes. She, the gentlest of creatures, stands ready to kill what the Doctor/Valeyard has become: the Mighty One, ruling the multiverse from Chronopolis.

'Doctor Who Unbound', the Alternate History and the Fannish Text
Karen Hellekson

As Mel seeks the Doctor, the Valeyard, accompanied by his cheerful yet morally ambiguous companion, Ellie Martin (Juliet Warner), visits the sites of the Doctor's former incarnations' meddling in an attempt to undo what he did, thus wiping away every trace of the Doctor. Logopolis, the Dalek home world, his initial meeting with Mel – all are engineered away, and with each erasure, the Valeyard forgets, even as listening fans remember: the Doctor was there, and the fan knows it, can identify down to the episode when the engagement occurred. The episode's synopsis at Big Finish's website summarizes it thus: 'Like dominoes, as one timeline falls, the others come cascading down around it. You can engineer new timelines, new possibilities but before long, the distinction between what is, what was, what might be and what never can be becomes blurred.'

The fannish text
With its textual doublings, its references to the *Trial of a Time Lord* serial, and its literal erasure of canon events, 'He Jests at Scars' has as its very theme the notion of alterity – that is, something radically other or alien. However, the intertextuality in this Unbound title goes beyond canon. The episode also refers to a number of spin-off *Doctor Who* novels and comics. One fan, Alden Bates, in his 'DiscContinuity guide', identifies the following:

The Diadem and Pakhars were introduced in the New Adventure *Legacy* [1994] by Gary Russell. The BBC book *Heritage* [2002], by Dale Smith. Mel's full name, history including her parents and date of birth come from the BBC book *Business Unusual* [1997], again by Gary Russell. Battle TARDISes first appeared in Steve Parkhouse's *DWM* [Doctor Who *Monthly*] comic strip *The Stockbridge Horror* (*DWM* 70–75). The term Grandfather Paradox is given meaning in *Alien Bodies* [1997] by Lawrence Miles. The implication that the Valeyard was in Whitechapel echoes [the] BBC book *Matrix* [[1998] by Mike Tucker and Robert Perry]. The Valeyard sees Chronopolis as the Doctor's ancestral home, from [Marc Platt's] *Lungbarrow* [1997]. Ellie is from Big Finish's Sarah Jane Smith range. The Doctor, Steven and Dodo were in Kiev in the [2001] BBC book *Bunker Soldiers* [by Martin Day].

As Bates's reading indicates, a deep, fannish knowledge is required to truly understand all the story's allusions and depths. In addition to the programme's large canon, there have been so many official spin-offs, the canonicity of which are uncertain, that it is difficult to be well read in the universe's milieu. Understanding the text requires the specialist knowledge of a dedicated fan, one who has internalized literally hundreds of novelizations, audio dramas, comics, and official and unofficial magazines. The fan integrates these ancillary texts into the reading of the text, thus creating meaning beyond the text itself.

The specialized knowledge required to understand 'He Jests at Scars', or any of the

Unbound audios, might be paralleled with the Doctor's specialized knowledge. The same might be said of the fan. In 'He Jests at Scars', the fan uses all the knowledge at her disposal to explicate the texts. The adventure unfolds, and the fannish mind makes sense of it by relating it to what is known (knowledge of canon and authorized spin-off texts, as Bates's listing above hints at) and what is unknown (the strategies to be used by the players in the situation to meet their goals). The fan creates something that incorporates all the bits of known information and synthesizes it into a whole: a metatext. She then applies this metatext to novel situations to understand them. For example, in 'He Jests at Scars', the fan must take what she knows of the character of Mel from canon, particularly the *Trial of a Time Lord* sequence, as well as the spin-off novels, then integrate all that information with the bitter Mel presented in the audio. How did one Mel turn into the other?

The ultimate end of the process of the creation of this metatext (as opposed to the metatext itself) is agency – the ability to bring about events – which in the case of 'He Jests at Scars' is conflated with understanding, because the reader-fan cannot of course literally act; she can only listen. The action occurs in the process of meaning making, and with that meaning comes the reward of pleasure. The fan uses her deep, hard-earned knowledge to construct an understanding of the new Mel presented to her. From textual clues, the fan knows that the bitter Mel has spent years looking for the Doctor and has even been assisted by the Time Lords. She feels guilt and despair after the Doctor lost his obviously rigged trial. These feelings have not only changed her, but have also caused her to throw in her lot with the Time Lords. The fan, like the Doctor, thus constructs an answer to a problem – here, the problem posted by the text of a changed Mel. Alas, this is not the case of Mel in the text itself. She fails to solve the problem. 'He Jests at Scars' ends badly. The Doctor is not redeemed, and Mel is not saved.

Conclusion

Every title in the Unbound series works to create a frisson in the listener, a moment of 'I know who that is', or 'Wait. That's not right. It didn't happen that way'. Each audio drama is a valentine to the fans, rewarding their deep canonical knowledge by creating alterations to canon and stepping back, as if to say, 'What do you make of this?' The answer is simple: fans use their extensive knowledge to create a meaning richer than that presented by the text itself, because of the effort and knowledge required to construct it. Fan professionals created the Unbound titles for well-read, educated fan listeners – for listeners like themselves.

Alternate history as a genre flips agency from impersonal historical forces or great men to the average individual and valorizes the work of the construction of the metatext required to understand the presented text. 'He Jests at Scars' notes that 'the distinction between what is, what was, what might be and what never can be becomes blurred', but this might just as well be said of the entire genre of the alternate history. ●

'*Doctor Who* Unbound', the Alternate History and the Fannish Text
Karen Hellekson

~~~~~~~~~

GO FURTHER

Books

The Alternate History: Refiguring Historical Time
Karen Hellekson
(Kent: Kent State University Press, 2001)

History That Never Happened: A Treatise on the Question, What Would Have Happened If ...?
Alexander Demandt
(Jefferson, NC: McFarland, 1993)

Extracts/Essays/Articles

'Why do we ask "what if?" Reflections on the function of alternate history'
Gavriel Rosenfeld
In *History and Theory*. 41: 4 (2002), pp. 90–103.

'Alternate history and postmodern temporality'
Paul Alkon
In Thomas R. Cleary (ed). *Time, Literature and the Arts: Essays in Honor of Samuel L. MacEy*
(Victoria, British Columbia, Canada: University of Victoria Department of English, 1994), pp. 65–85.

Film/Television

Doctor Who [Classic series], Sydney Newman and Verity Lambert, creators (London, UK: BBC, 1963)

Trial of a Time Lord:
The Mysterious Planet, Nicholas Mallett, dir. *Doctor Who* [Classic series] (London, UK: BBC: 1986)
Mindwarp, Ron Jones, dir. *Doctor Who* [Classic series] (London, UK: BBC: 1986)
Terror of the Vervoids, Chris Clough, dir. *Doctor Who* [Classic series] (London, UK: BBC: 1986)
The Ultimate Foe, Chris Clough, dir. *Doctor Who* [Classic series] (London, UK: BBC: 1986)
The War Games, David Maloney, dir. *Doctor Who* [Classic series] (London, UK: BBC: 1969)

Online
Websites

DiscContinuity guide, www.tetrap.com/drwho/disccon/

Big Finish Unbound, www.bigfinish.com/ranges/released/doctor-who---unbound
'TARDIS Index File' [*Doctor Who* wiki], tardis.wikia.com/wiki/

Audio
Table 1 **Summary of *Doctor Who* Unbound Big Finish Audio Dramas***

Title	Release Date	Director	Writer	What If ...	Doctor	Other Character
1. Auld Mortality	May 2003	Nicholas Briggs	Marc Platt	... the Doctor and Susan had never left Gallifrey?	Geoffrey Bayldon (alternate First Doctor)	Susan (Carole Anne Ford)
2. Sympathy for the Devil	June 2003	Gary Russell	Jonathan Clements	... the Doctor had not been UNIT's scientific advisor?	David Warner (alternate Third Doctor)	The Brigadier (Nicholas Courtney), the Master (Mark Gatiss)†
3. Full Fathom Five	July 2003	Jason Haigh-Ellery	David Bishop	... the Doctor believed the ends justified the means?	David Collings	—
4. He Jests at Scars	August 2003	Gary Russell	Gary Russell	... the Valeyard had won?	Michael Jayston (as the Valeyard, an alternate Sixth Doctor)	The Valeyard (Michael Jayston), Melanie Bush (Bonnie Langford)
5. Deadline	September 2003	Nicholas Briggs	Robert Shearman	... Doctor Who had never made it to television?	Derek Jacobi (as Martin Bannister)	Susan (Genevieve Swallow),† Barbara (Jacqueline King)†
6. Exile	October 2003	Nicholas Briggs	Nicholas Briggs	... the Doctor had escaped the justice of the Time Lords?	Arabella Weir (alternate Third Doctor)	—
7. A Storm of Angels (sequel to #1)	January 2005	John Ainsworth	Marc Platt	... the Doctor really had changed history, even just the tiniest bit?	Geoffrey Bayldon	Susan (Carole Anne Ford)
8. Masters of War (sequel to #2)	December 2008	Jason Haigh-Ellery	Eddie Robson	—	David Warner	The Brigadier (Nicholas Courtney), Davros (Terry Molloy)

* Compiled from information from Big Finish's *Unbound* website. The 'what if?'
statements are taken directly from the website.
† Actor did not originate the role.

Chapter 12

Doctor Who, Slacktivism and Social Media Fandom

Jeremy Sarachan

→ The success of the New *Doctor Who* series and the growth of social media occurred simultaneously, suggesting that the popularity of the show can be partly attributed to a larger *Doctor Who* narrative that includes blogs, online reviews, Facebook groups, Twitter feeds and even boards on Pinterest. According to the 5 November 2012 issue of *New York Magazine*, the official *Doctor Who* Facebook page had 2.7 million likes, the official Twitter account had 267,000 followers, and *Doctor Who* ranked ninth in a list of 'most devoted fan bases'.

With the emergence of these opportunities to engage with *Doctor Who*, has it become too easy to be a fan of the programme? A similar question arises in discussions about online activism. *Slacktivism* refers to the actions by social media activists whose so-called humanitarian actions ultimately require little effort. Such behaviours include liking a Facebook page sponsored by a non-profit or signing an online petition. This may lead to satisfaction for the individual, but ultimately requires no significant commitment or sacrifice and offers questionable value. The same accusations can be made towards twenty-first-century fandom. If the barriers to becoming a fan have fallen, what is the real difference between a fan and a typical viewer?

Before social media, fewer opportunities existed for fans to engage with the programme's producers or each other. One could attend *Doctor Who* conventions or join an organization like the *Doctor Who* Fan Club of America to receive a newsletter and physical memorabilia (e.g. buttons), but these options generally maintained a one-way information flow. Furthermore, broadcast times varied from city to city. Episodes premiered in the United States months or years after the original broadcasts in the United Kingdom, and in some cities, PBS stations scheduled the show late on weekend nights, resulting in frequently unsuccessful attempts to remain awake past midnight.

Interest in the show continued after the cancellation of the Classic series in 1989. *Doctor Who* Magazine (*DWM*) continued to publish, despite the lack of new episodes to discuss and review. Original *Doctor Who* novels from Virgin Books continued the narrative after the show's cancellation. Earlier books had focused on converting broadcast episodes into prose, but the 1990s saw the New Adventures series develop the Doctor's story further, while radio programmes produced by Big Finish offered complementary audio performances. However, except for the broadcast of the Fox *Doctor Who: The Movie* (Sax) in 1996, the majority of viewers had little ongoing connection with the Whoniverse.

Manipulating time and space

On-demand technologies now allow even the most casual viewers to redefine both the time and space in which they watch the New series. The traditional, stereotypic manner that describes how one might watch the show (hiding 'behind the sofa') takes on new meaning when a laptop or tablet allows one to be anywhere and watch at a personally convenient time. Previously one had to be purposely available during the broadcast, and the predictability of the schedule made the choice to watch habitual, defining the concept of 'appointment television'. Paradoxically, when viewers choose to watch *Doctor Who* away from a traditional setting (e.g. living room, early evening), the resituating of the apparatus used to view the programme demands that the audience make a greater commitment to watch. When viewers watch the programme at any time and any place, then the number of possible distractions multiplies – both in terms of viewing options and the opportunity to do something other than watching television. Given this vari-

Doctor Who, Slacktivism and Social Media Fandom
Jeremy Sarachan

ability, any *Doctor Who* viewer who makes a conscious and repeated choice to watch could be considered a fan.

Who isn't a fan? (The future of television)
Available technologies lead to greater control over the experiences created around the mythology of *Doctor Who*. Users can choose the extent that they wish to engage with the programme, by choosing to 'just' watch the show or to enhance the experience with other videos, games or social media discussions.

In this sense, the outdated limits placed on fans – waiting two years to watch the show on public broadcasting at a scheduled time without any other contact with online fiction or nonfiction conversations – no longer exist. In 2013, media consumption (especially for an American watching a British television import) typically requires action. As viewing habits come to rely on streaming media, the effort to find the show will become commonplace, and less worthwhile programming will be ignored.

Chris Anderson's concept of the long tail suggests that the small audience for all 'cult' programming equals the size of the large audience for a few popular shows. In this way, cult programmes may begin to erode the economic dominance of popular series, leading to financial success for niche programming. In summer 2012, the mainstream magazine *Entertainment Weekly* published a cover story on *Doctor Who* and other cult shows, while in December 2012, the programme won *TV Guide*'s 'Fan favourite' contest. This highly visible acknowledgement of programming like *Doctor Who* comes as a result of committed viewers whose actions can and should qualify them as fans.

Transmedia experiences
In the last decade, viewers have come to experience substantial access to *Who*-related information through social media and other sites that encourage user interaction. John Tulloch, who has written extensively about *Doctor Who*, suggests that an 'intertextual context' occurs in fan conversations. He interviewed fans about the show and found that they did not limit the conversation to one episode at a time, instead finding it preferable to make sense of specific events within the broader history of the programme and then relate that conversation to issues of gender, class and politics. Tulloch cites the political overtones of *The Monster of Peladon* (Mayne, 1974, Season 11) or the treatment of female companions as examples. Brigid Cherry of St Mary's University College analysed fans of the New series in terms of how they view the show (passively or interactively) and how they convey emotions virtually. She concludes that online interactions possess the same validity as face-to-face conversations.

Henry Jenkins, a professor at the University of Southern California who specializes in fan studies, offers this definition of transmedia storytelling (2011):

Transmedia storytelling represents a process where integral elements of a fiction get

Fig. 1: Brigadier Alistair
Gordon Lethbridge-Stewart
(Nicholas Courtney) makes
his last appearance in the
Doctor Who universe in The
Sarah Jane Adventures story
'Enemy of the Bane' (2008).
(The Sarah Jane Adventures
©BBC-Wales).

dispersed systematically across multiple delivery channels for the purpose of creating a unified and coordinated
entertainment experience. Ideally, each medium makes it
own unique contribution to the unfolding of the story.

Transmedia storytelling considers all media related to
the show (i.e. the television programme, blogs, Wikipedia
entries, video games, fanfiction and videos) as important
to the formation of the overall experience. This definition creates a framework for fans to become part of the
overall narrative and permits them to engage with the
mythology of the programme with the understanding and
appreciation that all elements – professional or amateur
productions or news and commentary from fans or jour-
nalistic sources – offer value and enhance engagement.
Additionally, overlapping characters between Doctor Who,
Torchwood (Davies, BBC, 2006–11) and The Sarah Jane Adventures (Davies, BBC, 2007–11) create what Jenkins labels
as radical intertextuality, or multiple perspectives within
the same fictional universe. For example, fans expressed

frustration that Nicholas Courtney (who played Brigadier Lethbridge-Stewart intermit-
tently on the Classic series from 1968 to 1989) did not appear on the New series, but
he ultimately made a guest appearance in The Sarah Jane Adventures a few months
before he passed away (Figure 1). Mirroring real life, Lethbridge-Stewart's death received a plot-significant mention in the Doctor Who episode, 'The Wedding of River
Song' (Webb, 2011, Series 6, Episode 13), and his daughter was introduced as a recurring
character in 'The Power of Three' (Mackinnon, 2012, Series 7, Episode 4).

Fig. 2: Amy, Rory, and their
adopted son, Anthony in
'P.S.' (2012), a storyboard
epilogue to 'The Angels Take
Manhattan' (2012), released
online by the BBC. (Doctor
Who ©BBC-Wales).

Jenkins explains that transmedia experiences also require multimodality: the story
unfolds in different media platforms in a manner appropriate to that interface. For example, a novel can offer more insight into the thoughts of the characters while a video
game can focus more on action, creating an immersive and interactive experience. Official BBC-sponsored webisodes can offer background narratives that don't fit within a
full episode. For example, 'Pond Life' (Metzstein, 2012) offers a glimpse into Amy and
Rory's life while the Doctor travels alone with a conclusion depicting their marital separation. Similarly, 'P.S.' (Chibnall, 2012), a video short presented as an animated storyboard with voice-over, reveals how Rory's dad, Brian, learns about Amy and his permanent displacement into the past (Figure 2).

Following this definition, the overall narrative of the Doctor's adventures becomes a
complex network of texts: the television programme, novels, radio programmes, comic
books and video games, along with user-generated fanfiction and fan videos, specula-

Doctor Who, Slacktivism and Social Media Fandom
Jeremy Sarachan

tive text and video discussions, and mashup videos exploring 'what might have been'. These media forms are discussed below.

Databases and folksonomies

Fanfiction has been written for decades, long before social media made it easy to share these works. Previously, fans distributed and traded fiction in person, at conventions or via regular mail. Now, sites like Doctor Who *FanFiction Archive* and *A Teaspoon and an Open Mind* offer fans the opportunity to write and read stories across genres that encompass romance, adventure and character studies. Other stories dramatize missing scenes and events positioned between existing episodes.

These sites demonstrate media theorist Lev Manovich's theory that new media narratives can be subsumed by database structures. Following this model, the stories collected in *A Teaspoon and an Open Mind* may be accessed by users who specifically choose a Doctor, secondary characters, genre and ratings. Readers also can review stories, encouraging dialogue between writer and reader. To facilitate these actions, folksonomic practices occur: folksonomies allow users to define their own categories, just as the Dewey Decimal System is used to catalogue library books. With the latter, established categories assigned to texts, media or objects establish a fixed organizational structure. With folksonomies, users continually redefine the organization, creating original tags reused by other users to gradually create a new and relevant system. Social bookmarking sites like Delicious use this technique to organize web links and online retailers like Amazon use it to organize customer interests.

Also following a database structure, the *Doctor Who* wiki *tardis.wikia.com* parallels the familiar format of Wikipedia to offer a user-created encyclopedia of information related to the programme. The editing capabilities of this wiki empower fans to create their own non-fiction texts that describe and make sense of the entire history of the show (focusing on the television programme, books, merchandise, and other professionally produced media).

Reviews and blogs

For *Doctor Who* fans seeking out discussion about the programme, the Internet facilitates the discovery of episodic-based reviews published in numerous professional and amateur publications, including *The Guardian*, a mainstream newspaper in the United Kingdom, and *denofgeek.com*, a popular website/blog about science fiction. Some of these sites publish two reviews for the same episode, one with and one without spoilers (details that give away too much of an episode's content). These sites encourage participation by allowing fans to comment on the reviews, resulting in detailed critiques of the aesthetics and plot logic of an episode, along with speculation about future stories. Blog rankings in Google matter greatly in terms of finding readers, and a low ranking makes it difficult for a new blog to find an audience. Consider that a search for 'Doctor

Fig. 3: Matt Smith, Arthur
Darvill, and Karen Gillan are
questioned by the audience
at Comic-Con 2012.
(©PCJonathan;
Doctor Who ©BBC).

Fig. 4: A still from
a machinima,
'The war menace'.
(©FoxHoundProductions;
Doctor Who ©BBC).

Who' and 'blog' leads to 47,600,000 results (as of this writing). Such comprehensive results makes it nearly impossible for any one blogger to have a significant readership, but makes it extremely easy for a reader to find specific blog posts about any given *Who*-related topic: considering David Tennant's final episode, a viewer searching for: '"Doctor Who" and "blog" and "Wilfred Mott" and "death scene"' will obtain 420 results.

Professional and amateur videos on YouTube

A search for 'Doctor Who' on YouTube leads to 1,260,000 videos. These offerings range from official BBC promotional video to user-created machinima. Specific categories include:

Promotional videos from the BBC that offer previews of upcoming series and interviews with the show's producers, writers and stars. This also includes appearances by the stars on celebrity talk shows and official interviews at recognized events like Comic Con. (For example, '*Doctor Who* at Comic Con 2012 (Part 1 of 5) Q&A Matt Smith, Arthur Darvill, and Karen Gillan') (Figure 3).

Illegal postings of episodes frequently uploaded in sections to comply with time limits. Copyright violations often lead to the removal of these videos.

Cinéma vérité-style footage of the television show being filmed or actor sightings, often recorded on smartphones.

User commentary of the programme or particular episodes in the form of a video blog recorded with a camera integrated into a desktop or laptop.

User-created *Doctor Who* narratives featuring writing, videography and editing by fans. This category includes live-action videos or machinima. The latter uses a video game or virtual world as a set and staging area, adding actor-controlled avatars to perform scenes visually, with voices and sound effects typically added in post-production; see '*Doctor Who* – The machinima series – Flight of fancy' or '*Doctor Who* | Series II | Episode 1 | "The war menace" (The movies machinima)' for two examples (Figure 4).

Mashups that remix footage from various *Who* episodes to create new stories, music videos, unofficial trailers, and newly conceived scenes. (Occasionally, scenes from other programmes may be used.) Examples include a trailer of a hypothetical David Tennant-era episode that brings back Romana and a music video of the Tenth Doctor/ Rose 'romance' synced to the Beatles's 'I feel fine' (Figure 5).

The audience numbers for these videos range from under one hundred to hundreds of thousands of views, and offer yet another method for viewers to connect to the show,

Doctor Who, Slacktivism and Social Media Fandom
Jeremy Sarachan

and more significantly, add to the ongoing narrative.

Social media and the network

In addition to the official *Doctor Who* Facebook page, numerous *Doctor Who* Facebook apps help fans answer questions like 'Which *Doctor Who* character are you?' or more specifically, 'Which Doctor are you?' Character-based pages exist, with over 70,000 Facebook users liking 'Captain Jack Harkness' and almost 20,000 fans committed to Amy Pond. A page purporting to be written by the fictional character River Song (written by a fan?) offers comments written in River's voice.

Similarly, multiple *Who*-related Twitter accounts exist. @Doctor_Who_News offers official information related to celebrity interviews, DVD releases, and trivia about the show. *@the_doctor_bot* Tweets periodic lines from the show's scripts, adopting the alias of a quoting robot. For even more varied insight into the Twitterosphere's opinion of the show, a basic search with the #DoctorWho hashtag offers Twitterers an up-to-date and constant feed of *Doctor Who* related Tweets as well as a list of potential Twitter users to follow.

For those fans with interests in imagery, a search for *Doctor Who* on the curating site Pinterest offers numerous 'boards' collecting visual material related to *Doctor Who* (Figures 6 and 7). The images 'pinned' include user-created posters and art, visual mashups, a significant amount of *Who* merchandise (especially action figures) and other *Who* creations, such as a full-sized shower that resembles a TARDIS.

With all of these options for creating and sharing, the question arises whether such contributions define a 'fan' or merely a 'viewer'.

Slacktivism and online behaviour

Slacktivism has been criticized for causing potential activists to perceive that their limited actions create value beyond reasonable expectations. In an article on National Public Radio (2008), journalist Nico Savidge commented, 'some people think that these symbolic acts create real change. Slacktivism may have replaced out right apathy, but often the only the only thing it changes is how active people think they are.'

The value of slacktivist-labelled behaviours was debated after the release of the

Fig. 7: Pinterest users collect and 'pin' official and user-created images from across the Web. (©Sean Matthew Leary; Doctor Who ©BBC).

KONY 2012 video in spring 2012. This video depicted crimes against children in Uganda committed by Joseph Kony. When this chapter was written, almost 100 million people had viewed the pseudo-documentary on YouTube. When critics cited a suspect timeline and a biased presentation, supporters of the video were accused of acting without considering its overall accuracy.

Similarly, the Susan G. Komen Network received criticism about encouraging slacktivism in the fight against breast cancer, but Laurie Gilmore Selleck of Cazenova College suggests that meaningful awareness may result from '[s]aving yogurt lids, selecting pink ribbon adorned products, wearing pink bracelets' and that this behaviour 'leads women to be more diligent about examination and mammography'.

In his article on global revolutions that have used social media, Stefano Passini of the University of Bologna suggests that despite disadvantages specific to social causes, social media activism can lead to a larger audience and help to minimize the effect of physical distance. Such advantages, at least, also define some of the positive effects that social media has on fan communities.

Social media professionals and authors Charlene Li and Josh Bernoff define seven levels of online participation: *creators* write blogs and create videos; *conversationalists* post updates on Twitter, Facebook and other social media; *critics* comment on others' blogs and videos; and *collectors* compile information (e.g. pinning images on Pinterest). Less participatory categories include *joiners*, who register for social media sites but may not participate any further; and *spectators*, who read and view blogs and videos. *Inactives* do not use the Internet for any purpose. If we assume that anyone who positively engages with the show on some level beyond watching the programme may consider him/herself a fan, then Li and Bernoff's categories suggest that a large percentage of viewers fall under this classification. Fans engaging at these various levels of commitment create the ecosystem for transmedia narratives to thrive.

On-demand options

Finally, rather than dismiss so-called *inactives* and others whose involvement with the show consists primarily of watching episodes, the efforts taken to view the programme may even require activity associated with fandom.

Prior to on-demand and even cable programming, American viewers had to wait years to see episodes on PBS (primarily) or occasionally view newer episodes screened at science fiction conventions. With the New series, BBC America broadcasts episodes on the same day as its United Kingdom premiere.

However, as entire seasons become available on DVD, and more notably, episodes of *Doctor Who* stream on Netflix and iTunes, viewers may collect these episodes. In the past, users could save videos of the programme by recording them on VHS tape – a

Doctor Who, Slacktivism and Social Media Fandom
Jeremy Sarachan

laborious task by today's standards. But now, fans that wish to engage in this specific form of curation (even without interest in alternative *Doctor Who* texts) can maintain and engage in repeated viewings, as any 'good' fan would do.

Fandom for everyone
Casual viewers more easily connect to fan practices. In the afterword of *Fandom: Identities and Communities in a Mediated World* (2007), Jenkins writes

[m]aybe [...] there is no longer a centralized or dominant culture against which subcultures define themselves. Maybe there is no typical media consumer against which the cultural otherness of the fan can be located. Perhaps we are all fans or perhaps none of us is.

Ultimately, online activities – commenting on Dalek-shaped cookies on Facebook, making videos with friends, or writing online reviews— create more opportunities for viewers to participate. While it may be easier to become a member of the fan community, the resulting increase in user-generated content leads to the creation of meaningful *Who*-related narratives, creating a richer transmedia experience. ●

GO FURTHER

Books

Groundswell: Winning in a World Transformed by Social Technologies
Charlene Li and Josh Bernoff
(Boston: Harvard Business Review Press, 2011)

The Language of New Media
Lev Manovich
(Cambridge: MIT Press, 2001)

Science Fiction Audiences: Watching Doctor Who *and* Star Trek
John Tulloch and Henry Jenkins
(London: Routledge, 1995)

Extracts/Essays/Articles

'Big love: The 25 most devoted fan bases'
Matt Stevens
New York Magazine. 5 November 2012, pp. 66–67.

'The Doctor is in'
Clark Collis
Entertainment Weekly. 3 August 2012, pp. 29–35.

'The Facebook and Twitter revolutions: Active participation in the 21st century'
Stefano Passini
In *Human Affairs*. 22: 3 (2012), pp. 301–12.

'Squee, retcon, fanwank and the not-we: Computer-mediated discourse and the online audience for nuwho'
Brigid Cherry
In In Christopher J. Hansen (ed). *Ruminations, Peregrinations, and Regenerations: A Critical Approach to Doctor Who* (Newcastle: Cambridge Scholars Publishing, 2010), pp. 209–32.

'Pretty in pink: The Susan G. Komen network and the branding of the breast cancer cause'
Laurie Gilmore Selleck
In *Nordic Journal of English Studies*. 9: 3 (2010), pp. 119–38.

'Afterward: The future of fandom'
Henry Jenkins
In Jonathan Gray, Cornel Sandvoss and C. Lee Harrington (eds). *Fandom: Identities and Communities in a Mediated World* (New York: New York University Press, 2007), pp. 357–64.

Film/Television

The Sarah Jane Adventures, Russell T. Davies, creator (Cardiff, UK: BBC, 2007)
Torchwood, Russell T. Davies, creator (Cardiff, UK: BBC, 2006)
Doctor Who [Classic series], Sydney Newman and Verity Lambert, creators (London, UK: BBC, 1963); [New series], Russell T. Davies, creator (Cardiff, UK: BBC, 2005)

'P.S.', Chris Chibnall, writer *Doctor Who* [New series, web/DVD extra], http://www.bbc.co.uk/programmes/p00zn6ff (Cardiff, UK: BBC, 2012)
'The Power of Three', Douglas Mackinnon, dir. *Doctor Who* [New series] (Cardiff, UK: BBC, 2012)
'Pond Life', Saul Metzstein, dir. *Doctor Who* [New series, mini-episodes], http://www.bbc.co.uk/programmes/p00y9ly3 (Cardiff, UK: BBC, 2012)
'The Wedding of River Song', Jeremy Web, dir. *Doctor Who* [New series] (Cardiff, UK:

Doctor Who, Slacktivism and Social Media Fandom
Jeremy Sarachan

BBC, 2011)
Doctor Who: The Movie, Geoffrey Sax, dir. *Doctor Who* [Classic series] (Hollywood, CA: Fox and London, UK: BBC, 1996)
The Monster of Peladon, Lennie Mayne, dir. *Doctor Who* [Classic series] (London, UK: BBC, 1974)

Online
Extracts/Essays/Articles

'*Doctor Who* wins *TV Guide* magazine's fan favorites cover contest'
Aubry D'Arminio
TV Guide. 4 December 2012, http://www.tvguide.com/News/Doctor-Who-TV-Guide-Magazine-1057095.aspx

'KONY 2012: What's the real story?'
Polly Curtis and Tom McCarthy
The Guardian. 8 March 2012, http://www.guardian.co.uk/politics/reality-check-with-polly-curtis/2012/mar/08/kony-2012-what-s-the-story

'Transmedia 202: Further reflections'
Henry Jenkins
Confessions of an Aca-Fan: The Official Weblog of Henry Jenkins, 2011, http://henryjenkins.org/2011/08/defining_transmedia_further_re.html

'The Long Tail'
Chris Anderson
Wired Magazine 12.10 (October 2004), http://www.wired.com/wired/archive/12.10/tail.html

Websites

Doctor Who at *The Guardian* [news and reviews], http://www.guardian.co.uk/tv-and-radio/doctor-who
Doctor Who at *Den of Geek*, http://www.denofgeek.com/tv/doctor-who/19457/doctor-who-at-den-of-geek
Doctor Who *Fanfiction Archive*, http://fanfiction.net/tv/Doctor-Who/.
A Teaspoon and an Open Mind, http://www.whofic.com/
Doctor Who at Facebook, https://www.facebook.com/DoctorWho?fref=ts
Pinterest; for one representative example, see: http://pinterest.com/seanmatthew/doctor-who-pins-they-re-more-like-a-big-ball-of-wi/

Tardis index file, http://tardis.wikia.com/wiki/Doctor_Who_Wiki
Doctor Who Official at Twitter, https://twitter.com/bbcdoctorwho

Other
Videos

'*Doctor Who* – I feel fine', 22 Sept 2008, http://www.youtube.com/watch?v=WOpkcYa8J_k&feature=relmfu

'*Doctor Who*: "Time hidden" Romana returns', 27 June 2008, http://www.youtube.com/watch?v=doYLkjQdXtA

'*Doctor Who* | Series II | Episode 1 | "The war menace" (The Movies Machinima)', 29 Jan 2012http://www.youtube.com/watch?v=6gFG4ZfhNqk

Doctor Who – The Machinima Series – Flight of Fancy, 19 June 2012, http://www.youtube.com/watch?v=jSE8L4zAK7k

'*Doctor Who* at Comic Con 2012 (Part 1 of 5) Q&A Matt Smith, Arthur Darvill, and Karen Gillan, 18 July 2012, http://www.youtube.com/watch?v=ExJRn0_XvFY

Radio

Day to Day (Slacktivism: Antidote to Apathy)
Hosted by Alex Chadwick
Los Angeles: National Public Radio, 11 September 2008.

Chapter
13

Gif Fics and the Rebloggable Canon of *SuperWhoLock*

Nistasha Perez

→ THE SUPER FANDOM OF *SUPERWHOLOCK*
A Time Lord walks into a bar and is met by two demon-hunting brothers and a detective. It's not the start of a dirty joke but instead the basic premise behind *SuperWhoLock*. In the grand tradition of fandom name smushing, *SuperWhoLock* represents the combined fandoms of *Supernatural* (Kripke, WB/CW, 2005–present), *Doctor Who* and *Sherlock* (Moffatt and Gatiss, BBC, 2010–present).

Doctor Who and *Sherlock* are BBC productions while *Supernatural* is an American series currently airing on the CW Network. Each series enjoys a loyal fan base with creative output in the form of fanfiction, fan art, fan videos, discussion and cosplay. Online, the social network Tumblr is a gathering spot for all three fandoms. Primarily image based, Tumblr allows users to post graphics, gifs, texts, videos, links and conversations. With Tumblr's reblog button, the site is an attractive social network option for fans by providing an easy way to spread fannish content and discussion.

SuperWhoLock may lack a definitive start date but once the idea of combining the fandoms was formed, Tumblr's focus on sharing allowed people to reblog the resulting creations with a push of a button. *SuperWhoLock* fans created fan art, fan videos, fanfiction, mock movie posters and gif fic. Gif, short for graphics interchange format, is an image type that allows for multiple layers in one image. When combined and played at speed, the images appear to be moving. In *SuperWhoLock*, gifs from all three shows are edited and combined with original subtitled dialogue to form gif fics. These gif fics become the wibbley-wobbly canon of *SuperWhoLock*. By looking at the ways television canon and the structure of Tumblr unite to create *SuperWhoLock*, this chapter explores how the combined fandoms of *Doctor Who*, *Sherlock* and *Supernatural* are changing fandom practices and creative fanworks.

How the Doctor and Metallicar make *SuperWhoLock* plausible
Through the combination of *Doctor Who*, *Sherlock* and *Supernatural*, fans are creating a crossover. Crossovers are fanworks that combine two or more media properties. In Henry Jenkins's canonical work *Textual Poachers* (1992), he categorizes crossovers as one of the ten ways fans rewrite television shows. Jenkins also notes, 'some series formats (*Doctor Who*, *Quantum Leap* [Bellisario, NBC, 1989–93]) lend themselves particularly well to cross-overs, since the primary texts already involve a constant dislocation of the protagonists.' By using the TARDIS the Doctor is able to travel to any point in time or space. Such freedom allows for not only a wide variety of television storylines, but also opportunities for fan creators. With the TARDIS and the Doctor's inquisitive nature, it's easy to see how a London crime or an American ghost story would interest the mad man with a box.

Based on Sir Arthur Conan Doyle's Sherlock Holmes novels, the BBC's 2010 adaption *Sherlock* follows the titular detective and his friend, army doctor John Watson, as they solve some of London's most peculiar crimes. Though only six episodes long (at the time of writing), *Sherlock* has a sizeable fan base that draws inspiration from the Doyle novels, other television adaptations and the feature films. *SuperWhoLock* fans however, primarily use the BBC's version of *Sherlock* when creating gif fics. Some of this preference is due to *Doctor Who* and *Sherlock* sharing writer and producer Steven Moffat. In addition, Mark Gatiss – who plays Mycroft on *Sherlock* – has written several episodes of *Doctor Who*. Although there has been discussion of an official crossover between *Sher-*

Gif Fics and the Rebloggable Canon of *SuperWhoLock*
Nistasha Perez

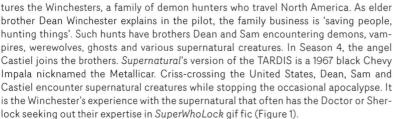

lock and *Doctor Who*, the technicalities of setting *Sherlock* in a world where alien invasions occur yearly has made the crossover unlikely to ever appear on television screens. On computer screens however, fans are able to send Sherlock on a variety of cases, including those involving disappearing police boxes or packs of werewolves.

Perhaps the odd man out, *Supernatural* is an American television show that premiered in 2005. The series features the Winchesters, a family of demon hunters who travel North America. As elder brother Dean Winchester explains in the pilot, the family business is 'saving people, hunting things'. Such hunts have brothers Dean and Sam encountering demons, vampires, werewolves, ghosts and various supernatural creatures. In Season 4, the angel Castiel joins the brothers. *Supernatural*'s version of the TARDIS is a 1967 black Chevy Impala nicknamed the Metallicar. Criss-crossing the United States, Dean, Sam and Castiel encounter supernatural creatures while stopping the occasional apocalypse. It is the Winchester's experience with the supernatural that often has the Doctor or Sherlock seeking out their expertise in *SuperWhoLock* gif fic (Figure 1).

At the core, all three shows are about discovery. *Doctor Who* discovers worlds and time periods beyond our own. The Winchester brothers discover how to vanquish supernatural creatures, while discovering who committed the crime is Sherlock's main motivation. The theme of discovery is so rich because the universes created by the shows are vast and full of history. Ironic as it is to say, none of these shows take place in a box. In Matt Hills's 'Defining cult TV' (2004), he notes that cult television 'make[s] fantastic worlds appear normal within a format and narrative structure'. The Doctor is an alien who has the ability to regenerate. Audiences have accepted this fantastic as normal due to repeated acts within the narrative. Likewise, Sherlock being the world's only consulting detective or the Winchesters fighting an army of demons is considered acceptable both within the canon and by viewers. Such fantastic themes draw the viewer in and offer tempting universes for fan artists to create in.

The three shows also contain a surprisingly small continuing cast. Although *Doctor Who* has had eleven Doctors and many companions, for any one season, the show often follows just two to three core characters. The small number of core characters allows fans to combine casts without overwhelming the author or the reader.

The small cast also makes it easy to bring in fans who want to enjoy *SuperWhoLock* but who do not watch all three shows. With Tumblr's reblog culture and visual nature, fans can begin to recognize key characters from popular shows as if through fandom osmosis. A person may not watch *Supernatural* but may recognize Castiel's trench coat because of photos or fan art. Similarly, one could not watch *Doctor Who* but could recognize the TARDIS as being a piece of science fiction history. This resulting one big fandom, where the lines between fandoms begin to blur, paves the way for super fandoms like *SuperWhoLock*.

Reblog, like, scroll, scroll, like, scroll, reblog

SuperWhoLock might not have become a widespread fandom phenomenon if not for Tumblr. As chronicled by Aja Romano in 'The demise of a social media platform: Tracking LiveJournal's demise' (2012), the blogging site LiveJournal was the main social site for fandom from 2002 to 2007. However, once the site changed leadership and those leaders arbitrarily deleted journal entries, fans lost their trust in LiveJournal and began looking for a new home. Tumblr soon became a hot spot for fandom.

If there's one thing fans excel at, it is sharing what they love. Sharing as a fan practice has increased the need for a simple and easy way to spread fannish content to friends and followers. Instead of dealing with photo hosting sites, html code and formatting, Tumblr users are able to click one button and share a post with their followers. These followers are then able to spread the image with one stroke of their keyboard. Such fandom practices allow users to share content to one's friends and friend of friends, and friends of those friends all across the Internet. In turn Tumblr users are exposed to their own friends' and friend of friends' interests. Tumblr's ability to spread varied interests and fandoms encourages multi-fandom participation amongst its users.

Like any social network, Tumblr has its usability pitfalls. Tags are inconsistent and depend upon uniform spelling. An unreliable tracking system makes Tumblr blogs like *SuperWhoLock*, *fuckyeahsuperwholock* and *asksuperwholock* gathering spots for the *SuperWhoLock* fandom. These sites accept submissions and reblogs within the *SuperWhoLock* universe and act as archives. Such communities are necessary for the creation, spread and enjoyment of *SuperWhoLock*. Unlike the represented series which air on broadcast networks, have an advertising budget and official websites, *SuperWhoLock* only has dedicated fans to maintain the community. Fans act as writers and artists who bring the narratives of *SuperWhoLock* to life. Maintainers of *SuperWhoLock* blogs act like television networks: they reblog and share the narrative with viewers.

SuperWhoLock has inspired a variety of fanworks. In the Tumblr user's *Mc-Steamy*'s fanvid '*SuperWhoLock* The Eleventh Reichenbach song trailer', the *SuperWhoLock* gang assembles to stop Moriarty from releasing Lucifer. There are 32 *SuperWhoLock* works on *Archive of Our Own* and 57 on *fanfiction.net*, two of the largest fanfiction archives. However, the majority of *SuperWhoLock* creations are graphic based. With neither archive specializing in graphics, most of *SuperWhoLock*'s canon can be found on Tumblr.

The evolution of fan narratives

If fandom existed within the Harry Potter universe, gif fics might be the most popular fan creation. Edited gif animations flow like Harry Potter's moving pictures, but a gif fic's purpose is to develop a narrative. Gifs are made from ripped video footage that is then edited in an image software programme before being exported in gif format. Gif

Gif Fics and the Rebloggable Canon of *SuperWhoLock*
Nistasha Perez

Fig. 2: The Master, Moriarty, and Lucifer meeting for tea and scheming. (Gif fic ©letmartyhandlethis Supernatural ©Wonderland; Doctor Who ©BBC; Sherlock ©BBC).

fics contain anywhere from one to ten gifs, with many containing either four or six to maintain the gif's symmetrical balance when uploaded to Tumblr. The number is enough to tell snippets of a story but not enough for the complex kind of storytelling found in an hour of television. With a limited number of gifs, exposition and set-up are often explained in an attached author note or left to the reader's imaginations.

Gif fics are not proprietary to the *SuperWhoLock* fandom. For example, at the *Arrows-and-duct-tape* Tumblr, gif fics chronicle Wade Wilson as he's recruited by the secret agency SHIELD. *SuperWhoLock* gif fics will even include other fandoms such as *Star Trek* (Roddenberry, CBS, 1966–69) or *Firefly* (Whedon, Fox, 2002).

Chosen scenes are not always the climax of a story; often the artist highlights bits of dialogue or moments in the story deemed especially amusing or particularly heartfelt. *SuperWhoLock*'s streamlined approach to storytelling lies in direct contrast to the complex narration found in *Doctor Who*, *Sherlock* and *Supernatural*. Whereas the television series have the luxury of an established medium and allocated time slot, *SuperWhoLock* artists have only their artistic skills and love of their fandom. *SuperWhoLock* artists have something the official series are lacking however; the freedom to combine such super fandoms without thinking of actor contracts, distribution rights or production details.

The one with all the villains
As Aja Romana notes in her *Daily Dot* article 'WTF is *SuperWhoLock*' (2012), *SuperWhoLock* 'usually involves saving the world from impending apocalypse, something so serious that it only makes sense to enlist as many superheroes as possible to stop it'. *Sherlock*'s Moriarty, *Supernatural*'s Lucifer, and *Doctor Who*'s Master joining forces is one such disaster waiting to happen. Such is the premise behind *letmartyhandlethis*'s black-and-white gif fic (Figure 2). A creator of several *SuperWhoLock* gif fics, *letmartyhandlethis* brings together *SuperWhoLock*'s worst villains for an unknown reason. Although the specific cause for their meeting is never revealed, Lucifer arriving in the last gif covered in blood, indicates the meeting is for more than just afternoon tea.

Prior to Lucifer arriving, the Master and Moriarty exchange pleasantries. Their greetings indicate they have met before, with Moriarty perhaps acting as a consulting criminal for one of the Master's plots. Or perhaps they met while shopping for suits. The importance is not on the specifics but the general idea of the men sharing a history. When Lucifer arrives, covered in blood splatter, the three villains can begin plotting. Their nefarious plot, whether to destroy the world's economy, release toxic gas, or simply remove all the cat videos from the Internet, is not revealed. Again, the details are not important. By creating the gif set, *letmartyhandlethis* has created a world where three

Fig. 3: The Winchester brothers are introduced to Sherlock Holmes and Sherlock's snark. (Gif fic ©Doomslock; Supernatural ©Wonderland; Doctor Who ©BBC; Sherlock ©BBC).

Fig. 4: (bottom) The Doctor and Sam enjoy their day at the office while John feels like he's done this all before. (Gif fic ©Cumberchameleon; Supernatural ©Wonderland; Doctor Who ©BBC; Sherlock ©BBC).

of the universe's most terrifying villains have decided to come together. The only way to combat such an unholy trinity would be to enlist the world's greatest heroes.

The one where Sherlock's wit meets the Winchesters'

In Tumblr-user *Doomslock*'s take on *SuperWhoLock*, the Winchester brothers find themselves both introduced to and insulted by Sherlock Holmes (Figure 3). Once the Doctor introduces Sherlock, Dean immediately recognizes the name from Arthur Conan Doyle's creations. Sherlock explains, with his trademark wit, that due to a parallel universe, he exists but the novels featuring him do not. With Sherlock Holmes being an internationally known character, whether he or the novels exist is one of the continuity problems that would plague any official crossover. With *SuperWhoLock* fan creations however, artists can individually choose how to resolve the issue or if they care to note it at all.

Sherlock also uses one of the Doctor's favourite phrases, 'spacey-wacey'. *Doomslock* gif fics employs a popular *SuperWhoLock* technique of having a character repeat a popular phrase or line from a series that is not their own. Sherlock's use of spacey-wacey indicates that he and the Doctor have met previously within the gif fic's canon while also further cementing the fusion of *Supernatural*, *Sherlock* and *Doctor Who*. The gif fic may only consist of one conversation, but it sets the tone for a continuing adventure.

The one where they go undercover

The gif fic artist *Cumberchameleon* captions her creation with '*Superwholock* (Part One) The Doctor persuades Sam and John to go undercover at an office in order to investigate the strange readings he's picked up, but Sherlock and Dean have other ideas' (Figure 4). Along with offering context for why the Doctor, John and Sam would be working in a non-descript office building, the caption also reveals that there are two other characters involved who are never seen within the gif fic. With a few lines, the author is able to expand the narrative beyond the six given gifs.

The final gif of John napping in an office chair provides not only a visual punch-

Gif Fics and the Rebloggable Canon of *SuperWhoLock*
Nistasha Perez

Fig. 5: John and Dean explore the TARDIS. (Gif fic ©Audreyii-fic; Supernatural ©Wonderland; Doctor Who ©BBC; Sherlock ©BBC).

line but also references Martin Freeman's earlier work in *The Office* (Gervais and Merchant, BBC, 2001–03). Referencing an actor's previous role is a way to add additional meaning to a shortened narrative.

The one where everyone gets lost
While on board the TARDIS, John and Dean happen upon very different rooms in *Audreyii-fic*'s gif set (Figure 5). John finds himself not in the library but at the swimming pool. Dean meanwhile is approached by a woman in red leather and matching devil horns. 'Hold on, are you in the Virtual Reality Room? No, no, no I just disinfected the controls from Jack's last visit!' the Doctor notes off-screen in *Audreyii-fic*'s caption.

Audreyii-fic, like the previous authors *Cumberchameleon* and *Doomslock*, uses colour to differentiate which lines come from which characters. The emphasis on clarity is important in a medium that relays on conversation but does not offer audio support. For example, in the third gif, only a swimming pool is pictured but the Doctor can still be heard asking John his location. The audience knows the Doctor's question is in yellow while John responds in white due to the two previous gifs assigning the colours to the characters.

Audreyii-fic has created multiple gif fics in this universe found in the tag #The Adventure of the Fixed Points Destinies. By marking all the fan creations with the same tag, *Audreyii-fic* is able to extend the narrative. In other adventures, Dean's and the Doctor's attempt to fix the TARDIS lands them on both the *Firefly* spaceship *Serenity* and *Star Trek*'s starship *Enterprise*. With proper tagging, a fan artist is not beholden to one gif set to tell a story, but instead is able to weave the narrative across multiple gif fics and create more complex narratives.

Fig. 6: SuperWhoLock AU. (Gif fic ©Monsieureames; Supernatural ©Wonderland; Sherlock ©BBC).

The one where Dean works for Moriarty
Consisting of six gifs, Tumblr-user Monsieureames's gif fic is an alternative universe example of *SuperWhoLock* (Figure 6). Free of any subtitled dialogue, the author's accompanying note explains the gif fic's exploration of a *SuperWhoLock* universe where Dean is not a hunter but a sniper:

{*Superwholock* AU} in which Dean works as a sniper for Jim, always accomplishing his assignments quick and efficient until one day, his task is a raggedy man named The Doctor. Dean shoots him, not knowing that the mad man with the blue box saw it coming and came up with a plan to fake his death.

Although the text is an alternative universe of a fan crossover, source material from all three shows is used. Moriarty baiting Sherlock in 'The Reichenbach Fall' (Haynes, 2012, Series 2, Episode 3) is repurposed to have Dean be the consulting criminal's victim. Like all gif fics, source material is repurposed for the sake of a new narration. Many fans can identify the last frame of the Doctor and Amy as having come from *Doctor Who*'s Series 6 episode 'The Impossible Astronaut' (Haynes, 2011, Episode 1). Although gif fics repurpose a scene for narrative effect, the creations do not strip away the emotional impact of original source material. There is no lessening of Amy's grief just because the shooter has changed. The viewer is still hit with the same emotional impact as when watching the episode. However, by staging a different narrative, fans are able to design a different universe.

The open universe of *SuperWhoLock*
SuperWhoLock does not have a strict canon. Since the crossover is a fan creation, there is no single writer, director, or powers-that-be to say what happened and what didn't happen. Such freedom creates an open universe for fans to work in, ones where Dean can be a sniper or characters are forced to go undercover. Open universes act as loose frameworks for fan creators who are then free to create their own unique canon: from a plethora of ideas comes unlimited universes.

Super fan narratives for a super fandom
SuperWhoLock is indeed a super fandom. As a combination of three of the most prolific online fandoms, *SuperWhoLock* has a large and talented fan base that is able to play with fantastic canon. At the same time, these fans are not beholden to one *SuperWhoLock* narrative thanks to the open universe aspect of *SuperWhoLock*. An open universe allows fans to create their own narratives through fan creations known as gif fics. Gif fics are meant to be seen in motion and, if interested, please check out some of these examples listed in the 'Go Further' section.

As an emerging fandom practice, gif fic norms are changing everyday. Some people employ colour-coded conversation; others tell the story in a comment box; with some preferring alternative universes. As upload limits increase and the practice spreads, more complex narratives can be written. Just as *SuperWhoLock* blends multiple television series, gif fics blend the conversation skills of a fanfic writer, the editing of a fan vidder, and the artistic skills of a fan artist to create fan narratives for a super fandom. ●

Gif Fics and the Rebloggable Canon of *SuperWhoLock*
Nistasha Perez

GO FURTHER

Books

Textual Poachers: Television Fans and Participatory Culture
Henry Jenkins
(New York: Routledge, 1992)

Extracts/Essays/Articles

'Defining cult TV: Texts, inter-texts, and fan audiences'
Matt Hills
In Robert Allen and Annette Hill (eds). *The Television Studies Reader* (London, UK:
Routledge, 2004), pp. 509–23.

Film/Television

Sherlock, Steven Moffat and Mark Gatiss, creators (Cardiff, UK: BBC, 2010)
Supernatural, Eric Kripke, creator (British Columbia, Canada: Warner Bros. Television, 2005)
Doctor Who [New series], Russell T. Davies, creator (Cardiff, UK: BBC, 2005)
Firefly, Joss Whedon, creator (Hollywood, CA: Fox, 2002)
The Office, Ricky Gervais and Stephen Merchant, creators (London, UK: BBC, 2001)
Quantum Leap, David Bellisario, creator (Hollywood, CA: NBC, 1989)
Star Trek, Gene Roddenberry, creator (Hollywood, CA: CBS, 1966)

'The Reichenbach Fall', Toby Haynes, dir. *Sherlock* (Cardiff, UK: BBC, 2012)
'The Impossible Astronaut', Toby Haynes, dir. *Doctor Who* [New series] (Cardiff, UK: BBC, 2011)

Online
Extracts/essays/articles

'WTF is *SuperWhoLock*?'
Aja Romano
Daily Dot. 5 October 2012, http://www.dailydot.com/entertainment/superwholock-
fandom-supernatural-sherlock/

'The demise of a social media platform: Tracking LiveJournal's demise'
Aja Romano
Daily Dot. 6 September 2012, http://www.dailydot.com/culture/livejournal-decline-
timeline

Websites

SuperWhoLock, www.superwholock.tumblr.com
Fuckyeahsuperwholock, www.fuckyeahsuperwholock.tumblr.com
Asksuperwholock, www.asksuperwholock.tumblr.com
'*SuperWhoLock*: The Eleventh Reichenbach song trailer', *Mc-Steamy*, www.mc-steamy.
tumblr.com/post/21678120186
Letmartyhandlethis, http://letmartyhandlethis.tumblr.com/post/15789862251
Audreyii-fic, http://audreyii-fic.tumblr.com/post/39471461415/hold-on-are-you-in-
the-virtual-reality-rec-room
Hunterlock, http://hunterlock.tumblr.com/tagged/@superwholock
Cumberchameleon, http://cumberchameleon.tumblr.com/post/41211481692/super-
wholock-part-one-the-doctor-persuades-sam
Doomslock, http://doomslock.tumblr.com/post/28125607672
Arrows-and-duct-tape, www.arrows-and-duct-tape.tumblr.com

Contributor Details

EDITOR

Paul Booth is Assistant Professor of Media and Cinema Studies in the College of Communication at DePaul University in Chicago, Illinois. He is the author of *Digital Fandom: New Media Studies* (Peter Lang, 2010), which examines fans of cult television programmes; *Time on TV: Temporal Displacement and Mashup Television* (Peter Lang, 2012) and the forthcoming *Media Play* (University of Iowa Press). Paul has published on *Doctor Who*, cult television, and media fandom in numerous outlets. He is currently enjoying a cup of tea and a biscuit.

CONTRIBUTORS

Brigid Cherry is Research Fellow in Communication, Culture and Creative Arts at St Mary's University College, Twickenham, UK. Her research focuses on horror cinema and fan cultures, particularly the female horror film audience. She has recently published work on horror-fan canons, feminine handicrafting in vampire fandom, projected interactivity in *Supernatural* and *Twilight* fanfiction and *Doctor Who* fans' responses to the return of the series. Her *Film Guidebook on Horror* was published by Routledge in 2009, is co-editor of *Twenty-First-Century Gothic* published by Cambridge Scholars Press in 2011, and has an edited collection on *True Blood* published by I.B. Tauris in 2012.

Katharina Freund recently completed her Ph.D. in digital communication at the University of Wollongong in Australia. Her dissertation analysed the online community of fan vidders, discussing how fanvids reimagine televisual texts. She now teaches communication and supports eLearning initiatives in her new role as a learning designer at the University of Wollongong.

Teresa Forde is Senior Lecturer in Film and Media at the University of Derby and Programme Leader for the MA Humanities and its pathway in Horror and Transgression. Teresa has recently published on the function of the soundtrack in science fiction film, addiction and technology in film and the construction of memory in television drama. She has also worked on science fiction literature, film and adaptation. Teresa's research interests include science fiction, individual and collective memory, soundtracks, gender, television drama, adaptation and experimental film.

Karen Hellekson is an independent scholar based out of Maine. She works in media, fan and science fiction studies. She entered fandom via *Doctor Who* in 1982.

Matt Hills is Professor in Film and TV Studies at Aberystwyth University, Wales. He is the author of five books, including *Fan Cultures* (Routledge, 2002) and *Triumph of a Time Lord: Regenerating* Doctor Who *in the Twenty-first Century* (I.B. Tauris, 2010). Matt has published widely on cult film/TV and media fandom, and is a regular reviewer for *doctorwhonews.net*. His next book is an edited collection for I.B. Tauris, *New Dimensions of* Doctor Who, due out in time for the show's 50th anniversary.

Craig Owen Jones is a Welsh-language lecturer for the Coleg Cymraeg Cenedlaethol at Bangor University, Wales. His research interests include Welsh popular music and cultural history, punk rock, science fiction studies, popular music in film and fandom studies. He has contributed articles to journals such as *Popular Music History* on subjects including hip-hop, underground music scenes and the logistics of the rock tour. He is currently completing a monograph on the history of Welsh-language rock music, to be published in 2014; a further book on *Doctor Who* is in the advanced planning stage.

Leslie McMurtry was born in Albuquerque, New Mexico and studied at the University of New Mexico and Swansea University in Wales. She has been published in *The Mythological Dimensions of* Doctor Who (Kitsune, 2010), *The Unsilent Library: Essays on the Russell T. Davies Era of the New* Doctor Who (Science Fiction Foundation, 2011) and Doctor Who *and Race* (Intellect, 2013), and edits *The Terrible Zodin* (http://doctorwhottz. blogspot.com). Her first radio play was recorded by Camino Real Productions, LLC, and broadcast in 2010. She lives in London.

Dylan Morris, an American proud nerd and recovering Anglophile, is a graduate student in Intellectual History at the University of Cambridge, UK, where he studies on a Paul Mellon Fellowship. Dylan researches cultural memory, national mythology, and nationalist rhetoric, with a focus on discourse about 'the West' in the twentieth-century American academy. He is a graduate of Yale University, where he wrote his undergraduate thesis on rhetorics of moderation and extremism in contemporary American politics. Dylan is deeply grateful to Fan Phenomena editor Paul Booth, to his interviewees, to his dissertation supervisor Joel Isaac, and to his family and friends for help and support in this project. When not writing about intellectual history or *Doctor Who*, Dylan can usually be found running, juggling or singing, though rarely at the same time.

Nistasha Perez has a background in graphic arts and Masters degree in Communication. Ever since stumbling across *Sailor Moon* in elementary school she's been interested in the ever-evolving world of fandom. She currently works in Washington D.C. and volunteers for the Organization for Transformative Works. Her online home is at *mediaopil.us*.

Ivan Phillips is Associate Dean of School (Learning and Teaching) in the School of Creative Arts at the University of Hertfordshire, UK, and Award Leader for both the BA (Hons) and MA Screen Cultures there. He completed his Ph.D. on the poetry of Paul Muldoon at the University of Wales, Swansea in 1998 and his research interests span such subjects as romanticism and its contexts, modernism into postmodernism, twentieth-century poetry and poetics and experimental fictions from Laurence Sterne to new media. He is currently contemplating the links between technology, poetry and the Gothic and is also pondering a new theory of media which he intends to call 'unsettlement'.

Jeremy Sarachan is Assistant Professor in the Department of Communication/Journalism and the director of the programme in Digital Cultures and Technologies at St John Fisher College in Rochester, New York. He has studied how social media and gaming influence parenting practices and the pedagogical uses of technology in communication courses, and now focuses his research on Internet memes and data visualization. He has published articles and essays in *Journalism & Mass Communication Educator, Journal of Interactive Learning Research, the International Journal of Learning and Media* and *In Media Res* and has published previous chapters on *Doctor Who* mashup videos, Facebook profile pictures and learning management systems and open-source philosophies. He would like to thank Reesha Quinones-Smith and other students in his Spring 2012 Emergent Media and Web Culture class for their writing and discussion about slacktivism.

Denise Vultee received her Ph.D. in English from the University of North Carolina at Chapel Hill. She is currently a lecturer in the Communication department at Wayne State University in Detroit, Michigan. Her research interests include metaphor, visual communication, media framing, digital humanities, social media and online teaching/learning. Her fascination with *Doctor Who* began in 1980, when she first encountered Tom Baker as the Fourth Doctor on American public television. She would go on to own a cat named 'Leela', and retains a fondness for long woolen scarves.

Richard Wallace is Associate Fellow in the Department of Film and Television Studies at the University of Warwick, UK. As well losing days in the archive researching missing British television programmes, his other research interests include film and television mockumentaries, music in/on film and television and changing practices in cinema exhibition. This research was conducted whilst Richard was a funded Early Career Research Fellow at the Institute of Advanced Study at the University of Warwick. Richard would also like to thank Jessica Hogg and the BBC's Written Archive Centre for help researching his chapter.

IN ALL MY TRAVELLINGS
THROUGHOUT THE UNIVERSE,
I HAVE BATTLED AGAINST
EVIL, AGAINST POWER-MAD
CONSPIRATORS.
I SHOULD HAVE STAYED HERE!
THE OLDEST CIVILIZATION:
DECADENT, DEGENERATE AND
ROTTEN TO THE CORE!
HA! POWER-MAD
CONSPIRATORS, DALEKS,
SONTARANS, CYBERMEN -
THEY'RE STILL IN THE NURSERY
COMPARED TO US!
TEN MILLION YEARS OF
ABSOLUTE POWER - THAT'S
WHAT IT TAKES TO BE
REALLY CORRUPT!

THE 6TH DOCTOR
THE ULTIMATE FOE

Image Credits

From *The Doctor Who Experience*
Inside covers

Additional Images

Introduction: Fig. 1 p.11 ©Gary Booth

Chapter 1:	Fig. 1 p.17 ©Ivan Phillips

Fig. 2 p.18 ©BBC from *An Unearthly Child* (dir. Warris Hussein)

Fig. 3 p.20 ©Marvel

Fig. 4 p.21 ©Susannah Leah from http://tardis.wikia.com/wiki/ File:Susannah_Leah_
TARDIS_console_design.jpg

Fig. 5 p.22 ©chairwithpanda.wordpress.com

Fig. 6 p.23 ©BBC-Wales from 'The Snowmen' (dir. Saul Metzstein)

Chapter 2:	Fig. 1 p.30 ©Joint Venture, ©Loose Cannon, and ©BBC from *The Underwater Menace*
(dir. Julia Smith)

Fig. 2 p.31 ©Change of Identity, ©Loose Cannon

Fig. 3 p.31 ©Joint Venture, ©Loose Cannon

Fig. 4 p.32 ©Joint Venture, ©Loose Cannon

Fig. 5 p.34 ©BBC from *The Ice Warriors* (dir. Derek Martinus), *The Tenth Planet*
(dir. Derek Martinus), *Marco Polo* (dir. Warris Hussein), and *The Invasion* (dir. Douglas Camfield)

Fig. 6 p.35 ©Change of Identity, ©drwhoanimator

Chapter 3:	Fig. 1 p.44 ©BBC/Fox from *The Movie* (dir. Geoffrey Sax

Fig. 2 p.46 ©BBC from *Scream of the Shalka* (dir. Wilson Milam)

Chapter 4:	Fig. 1 p.51 ©BBC-Wales from 'The Doctor, the Widow, and the Wardrobe'
(dir. Farren Blackburn)

Fig. 2 p.56 ©BBC-Wales from 'The Impossible Astronaut' (dir. Toby Haynes)

Chapter 5:	Fig. 1 p.63 ©BBC-Wales from *The Doctor Who Experience*

Fig. 2 p.65 ©BBC-Wales from *The Doctor Who Experience*

Fig. 3 p.68 ©BBC-Wales from *The Doctor Who Experience*

Chapter 6:	Fig. 1 p.73 ©Paul Booth

Chapter 7:	Fig. 1 p.85 ©Paulie Gilmore

Fig. 2 p.85 ©Private Lives

Fig. 3 p.85 ©Cheryl Whitfield Duval

Fig. 4 p.85 ©Hannah Rothman and Kaleigh Chambers

Chapter 8:	Screenshots ©BBC-Wales, *Doctor Who*

Figs. 1 and 2 p.99 ©raspberry_splatt

Figs. 3, 4 and 5 p.101 ©hollywoodgrrl

Figs. 6 and 7 p.102 ©sweetestdrain

Figs. 8, 9 and 10 p.103 ©sweetestdrain

DON'T SHOOT, DON'T SHOOT! I'M NICE.

THE 11TH DOCTOR
NIGHTMARE IN SILVER